The Teacher
as Expert

SUNY series, The Philosophy of Education
Philip L. Smith, editor

SUNY series, Teacher Preparation and Development
Alan R. Tom, editor

The Teacher
as Expert

A Theoretical and Historical Examination

Robert Welker

STATE UNIVERSITY OF NEW YORK PRESS

Published by
State University of New York Press, Albany

For information, address State University of New York
Press, State University Plaza, Albany, N.Y. 12246

Production by Dana Foote
Marketing by Theresa A. Swierzowski

Library of Congress Cataloging-in-Publication Data

Welker, Robert, 1950–
    The teacher as expert : a theoretical and historical examination /
Robert Welker.
        p.   cm.— (SUNY series, the philosophy of education) (SUNY
series, teacher preparation and development)
    Includes bibliographical references (p.) and index.
    ISBN 0–7914–0797–7 (alk. paper) . — ISBN 0–7914–0798–5 (pbk. :
alk. paper)
    1. Teachers—United States. I. Title. II. Series: SUNY series
in philosophy of education. III. Series: SUNY series in teacher
preparation and development.
LB1775.W425   1992
371.1'0023'73—dc20
                                                                90–49368
                                                                CIP

10 9 8 7 6 5 4 3 2 1

This book is dedicated to my wife Marilyn
and our four children Sonia, Joseph, John, and Susan.
Wonderful people.

Contents

One

Introduction

This book examines the phenomenon of expertise, especially as it relates to the understanding of the teaching craft. Many publications have either decried or celebrated the emergence of the expert as it applies to specific fields such as politics and medicine and as it applies to social affairs generally. Here we treat expertise as the basis for examining the practice of teaching. We look at two central questions. How appropriate is the concept of the teacher as an expert? What advantages or disadvantages does expertise present for teachers and the public they serve?

At the outset, an important distinction needs to be made with regard to the meaning of the word "expertise." In this work, expertise is conceived primarily as a sociological phenomenon rather than simply as a technical or scientific accomplishment. This means that expertise concerns human relations and moral and civic responsibilities as much as it does the accumulation of technical knowledge and skill. This has implications for our consideration of the expert as a central and indispensable figure in Western culture. An expert is more than a person who knows, he has become a focus of power and authority in our interactions with one another.

Ultimately and unavoidably, these understandings have had great bearing on how people have come to understand the field of education. As in other occupations, educators have continually asserted their particular competence in a specialized area of knowledge. They have repeatedly debated the technical skills required by the teacher's craft. Even more crucially, they have been concerned with the moral and social responsibilities of the teacher in the modern age. The question of whether regular classroom teachers should assert themselves as educational experts has rarely been faced directly until very recently.[1]

Nonetheless, as we shall see by examining the thought of a variety of educational leaders, the issues of expertise have been consistently raised. This work will argue that despite its many obvious advantages, the idea of the teacher as expert has certain limitations. It can be asserted only at some damage to a more public, inclusive, and moral understanding of a teacher's practice.

Toward an Understanding of Expertise

Before examining the connection between expertise and education, it is first important to come to a fuller understanding of the place of experts in contemporary life. While many have considered expertise in their examination of technology, Daniel Bell has perhaps provided the most exhaustive and direct analysis of expertise in his dispassionate description of the "postindustrial" society.[2] In searching for a starting point by which to judge the character of modern knowledge, Bell arbitrarily suggests the year 1788.

In that year the third edition of the *Encyclopedia Britannica* was published. For the first time, the editors of the work found it necessary to rely on specialists for information rather than on one or two men who took the "whole of human knowledge for their province."[3] It became more evident from that point, notes Bell, that knowledge had become fragmented and that no one would be able to master all the relevant information that one needed. In a famous dictum, Francis Bacon once asserted that knowledge is power. Bell adds that in the postindustrial age, it has also become a type of property.[4] As the economy shifts from the production of products to the production of services, more and more people rely on knowledge to make their living. Knowledge becomes part of the "social overhead investment of society."[5]

Most people think about the prominence of expertise in far less abstract and apocalyptic terms. It arises simply and naturally out of common experience, and out of the need to make sense of an evermore complex technical world. We will be concerned with a particular type of expert, the professional educator, yet experts abound in all areas of contemporary life. The reliance on them seems part of the very fabric of modern existence. The mechanic, the electrician, the small appliance repair person, and even the person who might style our hair or train our dog, can be considered experts.

John Kenneth Galbraith points out that in this general sense, experts are not extraordinary.[6] They are neither necessarily malicious nor beneficent. They are not geniuses, nor are they myopic specialists who have sacrificed common sense for a narrow view of the world. They are simply very useful people who have acquired a special knowledge that is not widely shared and that has allowed them to provide a service. It is this special knowledge that governs the patterns of dependence that mark our dealings with experts. Typically, we find ourselves deferring to experts because they know and we do not. Just as typically, we may be hard pressed to provide good and substantial reasons upon which to base our trust. As Thomas Haskell has understood the matter, we pride ourselves on our reasonableness and our independence and yet defer to experts, at times with as little grounds as the believer who defers to the Biblical account of creation.[7]

This does not mean, in any sense, that the modern reliance on experts lacks all rational explanation. It's just that in the rush of current events, few have the time or the training to check on expert decisions. Bell asserts that the very tenor of life has changed in the modern age, that lives have become more complex, and that common sense and common knowledge cannot solve all our problems. The economy is marked by an unprecedented division of labor, and technical knowledge has exploded fantastically. Theodore Caplow traces such an explosion through the number of specializations that have grown in the academic disciplines and in the labor force overall.[8] Bell notes the growth in library acquisitions and the vast increase in the number of publications that serve such specialties.[9] Others have noted the exponential increase in information, particularly in the sciences. In any case, such growth indicates on the larger scale a greater breadth of human knowledge. On the individual level, it indicates a narrowing of perspective and the need to depend on those who have confined their vision to a particular area of concern.

All of this might be more understandable and less overwhelming if the nature of social relations weren't so affected. For example, it seems impossible not to recognize the ironic obscurity and mystery that has attended the increase in scientific and technical knowledge and the growth in specialization.[10] Jobs have become so specifically defined that it is difficult for people to tell others exactly what they do.[11] It is more difficult for workers to understand or take responsibility for a larger product, and it is more difficult for people to see themselves affecting the huge bureaucracies that mark modern life. Finally, and perhaps most symbolically, most people seem to have little understanding of the most basic scientific principles, and they have only the most cursory understanding of the technical innovations and conveniences that they use each day. In one poll, not one person in ten could describe anything about how telephones work, and fewer still understood the operation of televisions.[12] In another recent study, only about one in twenty American adults could answer such basic questions as whether the earth revolves around the sun, whether antibiotics kill viruses, and whether astrology is scientific.[13]

This very incomprehensibility, of course, gives experts their reason for service and provides them with a livelihood. Yet the long understood values of independence and self-reliance are affected as well. Expertise helps make self-sufficiency something of an archaic virtue. Paul Goodman once described the modern dependence on technology by pointing to the helplessness of most people in matters of simple repair. Technology that adds such depth of understanding to our existence, that allows us to see into farthest space and into the microscopic depths of organic life can also carry with it a form of incipient blindness. The dependence on expert services gives access to care that is beyond personal ability. Yet a certain disability is always implied. As C. S. Lewis once put it, "If I pay you to carry me, I am not therefore a strong man."[14]

The Ambiguous Limits of Expertise

It may be too easy to criticize technological dependence and too easy to blame the expert. As will become evident throughout this study, these matters are never easy to decide. Many times dependence is justified. Some philosophers have noted that expertise has drastically changed the very nature of intelligence.[15] If intelligence formerly meant the ability of people to call on personal resources, experience, imagination, and ingenuity to deal with the unexpected, it now includes the judgment necessary to know when to consult the appropriate experts. The matter has moral repercussions. The person who attempts to repair a television without adequate knowledge is simply being foolish. The person who attempts to minister to the health of a vulnerable patient without adequate knowledge is being morally irresponsible.[16]

Nonetheless many have begun to question whether relations built around expertise are always appropriate or kept within reasonable limits. The dependency on experts hints at a lack of participation on the part of the wider public, as well as a passivity that might be as much a result of public indolence and apathy as the result of the widespread intrusions of professional care. When the matter calls for active public involvement or when the credentials of the expert become a mask for special privilege, then expertise appears to be more of a problem than a solution. An expertise that relies on technical explanation may overlook the moral and public nature of problems, substituting a technical strategy in the place of political or communal intervention.

This has caused more controversy in some fields than others. Politics has been one area in particular where the reliance on experts has received widespread attention. Frank Fischer, Ralph Lapp, Langdon Winner, and others have explored the idea of a "new class" of technicians and intellectuals.[17] Here the predominance of experts is commonly regarded as a threat to the democratic idea of public accountability. To depend more on an elite class of specialists is to trust less in the ability of the public to make governmental decisions. Others respond with a more hopeful conception. In Zbigniew Brzezinski's description of an expert-guided "technetronic society," the experts take over the management of social and political affairs.[18] The wider populace meanwhile is afforded the opportunity to cultivate more leisurely, cultural pursuits. Brzezinski's description follows the familiar historic pattern of technocratic thinking. The basic concepts underlying the technocratic conceptions of government we owe primarily to the French philosophers, St. Simon and his disciple Auguste Comte. Yet it is in the United States that technocratic conceptions of government have received a wide public hearing.[19] This reflects the ambivalent attitude of Americans toward technology and toward the control and efficiency it promises in all aspects of human affairs.

Medicine has been another area in which the phenomenon of expertise has raised perplexing problems. Medical knowledge is commonly crowned as the ultimate glory of technical expertise. Yet it is easy to forget how recent have been most of the technical innovations that have served to promote medicine as the prototype of all professions. Now that place of preeminence is being questioned.[20] Ivan Illich points out that many of the benefits of modern existence — increased life expectancy and elimination of many life-threatening illnesses — have come less as the result of medical intervention than as the result of modern sewage and water treatment techniques and a higher standard of living.[21] Issues surrounding the monopoly of the medical profession have arisen, particularly as it affects the ability of nontraditional healers to practice and the ability of patients to assume a more active role in their own treatment.

Again, these issues are never easy to decide in general. If there is one case in which patients have sacrificed their autonomy for a dubious cure, there are other cases in which a willful individualism has stood in the way of competent treatment. In *Anatomy of an Illness*, for example, Norman Cousins celebrates medical partnerships as a way to break down the authoritarian relationships that sometimes exist between expert doctors and passive patients. It was a partnership with a sensitive and caring doctor that allowed Cousins to find a personal cure for his debilitating illness.[22] He criticizes the docility of patients who want to be "fixed up like a car." Yet what of those illnesses that need the technique of the doctor and require their disinterested care? A few years later, Susan Sontag described her battle with cancer.[23] She was an unusually enterprising and intellectually gifted patient, yet she found herself contemplating her guilt over being afflicted with the disease. Her will had been sapped by a kind of self-blame growing out of the idea that cancer was a moral and spiritual judgment on her character. She found that taking personal responsibility for her illness only prevented her from seeking adequate help. Her subsequent book laments the public disposition to turn all medical ailments into types of moral judgments, thereby denying the afflicted the will to seek competent technical care.

Even malpractice suits, which indicate the general disposition of the public to question the heightened pretentions of professional competence, seem to carry a dual message. Some observers have understood malpractice suits to be another aspect of an increased public mistrust of the expert that began in the 1960s with student demonstrations in the colleges and with greater consumer activism.[24] Yet a closer look at the malpractice crisis, particularly as it affected the medical profession, reveals that most suits occur in precisely those areas in which technical knowledge is the most recent and therefore the most tentative.[25] Still the public demands treatment. All malpractice suits, whether merited or not, point out that people continue to rely on experts. They provide prima facie evidence that responsibility and blame are located elsewhere. Far from indicating a revived sense of public self-reliance, the great increase in malpractice claims may indicate a greater expectation being placed on experts and the increased disposition of the public to have its burgeoning need for comfort and satisfaction indulged.

Expertise and Education

These matters do not become easier to resolve within the field of education, although they may be more crucial. Expertise and education are integrally connected. Universalized schooling has been seen as instrumental in providing the common person a more secure sense of his own competence. Schooling indicates, on the one hand, an abiding faith in education as the means to equality of opportunity and as a means to weaken and even destroy the practice of privilege. On the other hand, schools act as sorting agencies in selecting those destined for different occupations and for those elite professions that have gained great status in modern life. In this latter sense, schools are the breeding grounds of the expert, the places in which specialists gain that rarified knowledge that sets them apart from the common layperson and that provides them with social wealth and power. In this way, schools may serve less to destroy classes of professional elites than to create them.

Schools themselves have increasingly become the locus of expertise. This book will center on the practice and status of the ordinary classroom teacher, but it is important to note that as schools have become more centralized, there has been a corresponding growth in specialization. Much of that growth has occurred in administration and administrative staff. According to the *Digest of Educational Statistics*, in 1920 there was one supervisor for every thirty-one teachers. By 1930, that number had increased to a supervisor for every twenty-two teachers, and by 1974 the number had increased to one for every sixteen teachers.[26] In 1985, there was one administrative staff person, including building principals and assistant prinicipals, for every eleven teachers.[27] Joel Spring points that this expansion reflects not only the growth in the field of administration as a profession, but also the growth in the number of people to whom the teacher must answer.[28] Expertise, in this sense, indicates not only particular competence but a sense of authority, power, and control.

Recent evidence suggests that teachers also are increasingly opting for specialization. The original specialties in teaching occurred as schools became segregated by age and grade and as junior high and high school teachers became responsible for a specific subject matter. But the modern growth in specialty is more narrow and seemingly more connected to the search for professional status.[29] The major development has occurred in the area of special education—teaching of the mentally retarded, the physically handicapped, the emotionally disturbed, and the learning disabled. Specialities have also arisen in reading and math as schools have moved to meet the needs of disadvantaged learners through remedial instruction. Early childhood education and bilingual education claim two other groups of specialists, and a smaller number of teachers have been working especially with the gifted. Stephen Kerr notes that in the sixteen-year period preceding 1980, the number of students opting for specialties rather than regular classroom teaching increased 1,000 percent.[30] Even as the number of employed teachers grew very little, if at all, between 1980 and 1985, the number of special education teachers grew 17 percent.[31] Compared to the number of classroom teachers, the number of teaching specialists is still small, but the drastic increase indicates that a movement is afoot that cannot be explained simply by the entitlement programs that encouraged the growth of specializations over that timeframe.[32]

The movement suggests that teachers have begun in earnest to follow the path that has led to the growth of professionalism in other occupations. The process involves the claim by a body of specialists to competence and exclusive jurisdiction over a certain field. The growth in specialties is one way individuals within an occupation can begin to assert their restricted right to practice and begin to claim for themselves the appropriate economic and social rewards befitting an exclusive profession. Kerr points to statistics that indicate that already the average salary for educational specialists exceeds that of the regular classroom teacher. He points also to more disturbing evidence that indicates that generalists are concerned with the encroachment of specialists upon their territory and fear the specialists' power to determine where a child should be placed or what education is appropriate.[33]

While these latter issues may be significant, they are not our direct concern. I believe that more significant questions are raised by the effect of specialty on how the practice of teaching is conceived. These concerns arise out of the limits of expertise discussed above. For if specialization wins for teachers the public regard and economic standing they have historically lacked, it may do so at the risk of falling into the same traps of technological dependency and public apathy that have been associated with expert relations in other fields. Teaching also could come to be seen in a more technical light rather than as a field particularly dependent on decisions made about the social ends of education. Especially in the United States, where faith in a publicly controlled education resembles a national church, the questions of whether the professions are self-serving, whether social problems can be solved through technical means, and whether public participation can be nurtured and preserved gain more importance.

Expertise and the Reform Movement

These kinds of questions now appear timely. They have recently received added emphasis from the widespread public criticism that has surrounded education. Despite the public outcry, it is not clear that the general adult community feels a more urgent need to take part in the educational process. The burdens of two-income and one-parent families stand in the way of such an eventuality. In addition, the current criticism surrounding schools appears likely to reinforce the belief in specialists and schools as agents especially capable of assuming educational responsibility. Professional educators have taken the urgent and apocalyptic tone of many of the reports criticizing schools and used it as a catalyst for reform in the profession. In this way, educational criticism might be seen as symbolically akin to the rationale for all expert intervention. "We are a nation at risk," began the report of the National Commission for Excellence in Education. "If an unfriendly foreign power had attempted to impose on America the mediocre educational performance that exists today, we might well have viewed it as an act of war."[34] One reasonable and typically modern way to deal with such a massive and overwhelming threat is to rely on more expert assistance.

Increasingly the teacher has become the center of the reform movement. Many reports have pointed out that it will take a more elite teacher corps to solve the problems of the school systems. The two most influential of the reports have been *Tomorrow's Teachers: A Report of the Holmes Group*, published in April, 1986, and *A Nation Prepared: Teachers for the 21st Century*, published the following month.[35] The reports included different participants. *Tomorrow's Teachers* was the work of a group of deans of education colleges who adopted the name of the Holmes Group in honor of Henry W. Holmes, an early reformer in education. *A Nation Prepared* was sponsored by the Carnegie Forum on Education and the Economy and included leaders of the major teachers' unions as well as a variety of professional and business leaders. Neither group included classroom teachers in their working group, though their major recommendations center on the position of the teacher in the academic community.

Basically, the recommendations of the two reports are similar and are justified in similar ways. Both reports wish to increase the prestige and the autonomy of the classroom teacher by making it a more exclusive profession. Each would abolish undergraduate education programs in favor of graduate teacher training, and each would apply more stringent and uniform standards for entering the profession. The Carnegie report urges the development of a professional standards board, while the Holmes Group emphasizes the creation and implementation of a series of tests for prospective teachers. Both groups recommend that teaching become more specialized through the adoption of a more differentiated ranking within the corps of teachers. In the Holmes Group's more elaborate recommendation, the teaching corps would be formed by a hierarchical structure that would include the career professional, the professional teacher, and the instructor. Each position would have its separate responsibilities and be charged by a

particular type of license that would give the higher levels of the occupation more professional responsibility and power.[36]

These reports do not simply recommend changes without putting
into place the mechanisms needed to realize reform. The Holmes
Group has increased its original membership to nearly 100 different
institutions preparing teachers. Many universities have already
increased requirements, and many others, even while facing insituti-
tional roadblocks, are presently putting into place postbaccalaureate
teacher preparation programs.[37] The Carnegie Corporation has funded
the development of the National Board for Professional Teaching Standards, which includes sixty-four members and which hopes that the
national board exam will soon be in place.[38] This multifaceted test will
certify that teachers possess the esoteric, specialized knowledge and
skill required of the expert practitioner. The direction and intention of
this reform effort is clear. Teachers need to be more professional, they
need to be better trained, they need to be equipped with the latest tactics that have been proven to be effective in the schools, and they need
to be empowered with the responsibility to employ what they know. In
this pursuit after more technical power, more autonomy, and more public respect and social status, teachers will follow the path of other elite
professions. As many see it, teachers will become more like doctors.[39]
They will assert their control of a well-defined knowledge base that will
not only demonstrate their technical abilities, but will pluck for them
the same rose of economic benefit that doctors plucked out of the nettle
of social criticism that engulfed the medical profession at the turn of
the century.

Again, this line of thinking raises many questions pertinent to our
investigation. The implicit assumption in the reform reports is that
teaching is to be founded on a more scientific, more expert basis. The
beguiling promise of expertise is that the same standardized and calculated methods that worked to harness natural forces can be used to
mold and direct human potential, including the human potential of
both teachers and students.[40] A prime question raised by the very concept of the teacher as expert is whether there exists in the immense
research on teaching anything resembling a science or giving evidence
to the idea that there is one best way to practice. The question ultimately reflects on whether teachers can or should be considered full
professionals in the exclusive and technical sense of the term—people
whose vocation is more formed by their competence than their character, more dependent on legal jurisdiction than human relation.

Finally, and perhaps most importantly, the issue of the moral
nature of a teacher's practice is raised. This issue has particularly

affected historical thinking about the role of teachers and thus will also be a particular issue here. Within this question, the appropriateness of conceiving of the teacher as an expert gains a more practical context. It is not altogether clear that the transition of teachers to the role of expert, "specialist in charge of education," can be as smooth as the transition doctors have made to the role of expert, "specialists in charge of health." First, there is the obvious need for parents to be integrally involved in the education of their children. Second, it is not clear that teachers can ever be like doctors in the social responsibilities of their role. Both doctors and teachers have strong historical connections to religion and to the priesthood. This connection served to imbue the two roles with certain moral constraints which indicated that character and moral bearing were as important to being a doctor or a teacher as was technical skill. For many reasons, doctors now have difficulty holding moral concerns at the forefront of their practice. (Indeed, it might be said that for the more technical medical specialties, it is possible to consider quality of service without giving much thought to any moral considerations whatsoever.[41]) We expect of the surgeon more a steady hand than a kind heart; it has become questionable whether a good doctor necessarily has to be a good person. The matter appears more problematic when considering the character of the teacher. It is hoped that the theoretical and historical investigation of this issue might yield additional insight.

Nature of the Study

We can now elaborate more clearly on the particulars of this examination of expertise and teaching. Immediately we should note the huge nature of this issue. We could easily pursue a much fuller exposition by examining more carefully the place of the expert in the modern world, the technical intrusion of expertise in such matters as testing and programmed learning, and the historical record of the schools in adopting technocratic solutions to political and moral problems. Raymond Callahan, Randall Collins, and David Tyack have already done some of that work.[42]

This work takes a more personal and more eclectic approach. As briefly noted above, we are generally seeking insights about the effects of educational expertise through an analysis of the thoughts and writings of some of our most prominent educational thinkers. This search is not a simple matter, because few educational theorists have viewed expertise as a direct concern. Nonetheless, the issues of expertise—the political and public nature of schooling, the monopoly of education, and the professionalization of teaching—are where we seek to be enlightened.

Chapter Two begins the examination with an analysis of expertise as conceived in the progressive era. David Tyack has noted that the progressive education movement contained different strands, and Chapter Two will attempt to review two of the strands in the thought of Ellwood Patterson Cubberley and George S. Counts. Cubberley led a group of educators whom Tyack refers to as administrative progressives. Counts was a leading social reconstructionist. Both thinkers had different ideas about the practice of teaching, particularly with regard to the place of technical knowledge and social obligation in informing a teacher's duties. This raised questions about who should have power and control over the schools. In the conflict between the views of Cubberley and Counts and in a concluding examination of the ideas of Jane Addams we face for the first time the limitations of reserving educational decisions to the province of a special group.

Chapter Three examines expertise as an aspect of professionalism. Two of the most prominent sociological studies of teaching, written by Willard Waller and Daniel Lortie, will be analyzed in this chapter. Lortie, worried about the development of a technical subculture, advocates a more exclusive profession. Waller, worried about the restriction of a teacher's role in a highly structured institution, advocates a more open concept of a teacher's practice. In many ways it is possible to see Lortie as a proponent of the teacher–expert and Waller as an opponent. Questions are raised about each of their views.

Chapter Four examines the origins and thinking of many of the leaders of the "romantic" movement in education. Focusing on the thought of several of the modern romantics, particularly Ivan Illich, the idea of the teacher as expert is directly confronted, particularly because it has seemed so diametrically opposed to the romantic view of the teaching practice. Nonetheless, as the examination of Illich hopes to make clear, the romantic idea of individualism is in many ways consistent with the idea of individualism that underlies expertise. This suggests that theoretically the positions of those approving or disapproving of a more scientific and exclusive teaching profession may not be that far apart.

The final two chapters bring the discussion into the modern era with a brief review of some of the current debate about the liberal and the technical in the practice of teachers. The recent work of Philip Jackson and Alan Tom will be reviewed, and the thought of Maxine Greene and Henry Giroux will be analyzed. These thinkers have begun to question the concept of expertise most directly. They have seen in expertise an abandonment of moral and social responsibility for the patriarchal language of technical competence. Greene and Giroux especially have seen the professionalization project as another aspect of hegemony, the project of the powerful to determine cultural legitimacy and the language of dominance. Despite the harshness of this criticism, it is clear that such ideas have a history and follow in many ways the thought of theorists previously examined. Yet they attempt to move beyond the past, to understand the practice of teaching in a more cooperative, interactive, and interdependent manner. Their ideas suggest ways to overcome the excessively technical and dominant concept of the teacher as expert.

Two

Expertise in Progressive Thought

The modern faith in the expert has its origins in the nineteenth century. It is closely tied to the rise of the professions and the increasing credibility of the sciences. It has also depended, in a certain sense, on economic prosperity. As per capita incomes have risen, vast numbers of people have been able to earn a living by providing a service, rather than being involved in the production of food. Until the end of the nineteenth century, such people would not even have been called experts, with all the word now implies, nor would they have been given the special credibility and trust experts are now afforded.[1] Such trust only arose with the increasing reliance on technology as a way of promoting progress and as a way of organizing a new, more efficient world. The enthusiasm and respect for the accomplishments of technology changed occupational conceptions and reoriented conceptions about ways to survive and succeed. As one exuberant writer put the matter, "Knowledge has become power. The first and most important industry of this new civilization is to cultivate brains."[2]

Occupational distinctions drawn along formalized lines indicate an increasing reliance on institutions and organizations as mediators to service. Experts require not only specialized training to set them apart from the lay public, but special places to practice. In the nineteenth century schools, hospitals, courtrooms, and even professional baseball parks became increasingly identified as loci of professional authority and competence.[3] The emergence of the expert went hand in hand with the emergence of professional organizations meant to protect and manage the interests of the new occupational elites.[4] As always, these shifts in social structure were marked by shifts in language. Professionals began to share special words, and old words took on new meanings to promote the reliance of the public on experts. Citizens became "clients" in a dependent relationship with their professional patrons, and a "lay-man," who once was subservient to the church, was now understood to be subservient to all those with special knowledge and training. An amateur, once commended as someone who pursued something for the love of it, now came to be known as someone who lacked the knowl-edge and skill to perform adequately.[5] In this way inferiority of skill could not be easily overcome by superiority of motive and character.

The early historical movement to identify the teacher as an expert faced this question: How could teaching be advanced as an occupation requiring specific technical abilities without losing its moral and reli-gious foundation? As expertise became solidly established as the basis for other professions, teachers sought to ground their craft in the authority of science without losing the sentimental, nourishing lan-guage and energy of the true amateur. This latter focus was indicative of the close connection between teaching and the ministry and a gener-alized Protestantism that was part of the common school movement and the evangelical zeal with which it was pursued. The self-image of the nineteenth-century educational leader was born more of the church than of the laboratory. Most of the educational crusaders of the com-mon school movement had fluid careers; few had picked education as a lifelong profession. Almost all, like Horace Mann who led them, were deeply religious men and very talented amateurs.[6]

This religious grounding was consistent with the popular view of the teacher. From the beginning, teaching was seen as a type of calling. Early normal schools emphasized the passion and focus of this calling even as they asserted, consistent with the trends of the time, that edu-cation was based on scientific principles.[7] Normal schools provided opportunities to a class of people who had limited chance for advanced education and for professional opportunities elsewhere. Women began to dominate the teaching field, especially in the elementary schools, not only because of lack of other career opportunities but also because many saw the female as more morally upright and constant. Teaching itself, fueled by the enthusiasm over Pestalozzian methods, was seen as a maternal and motherly occupation. In the words of Joel Spring, the school marm became the heroine of the common school movement.[8]

By the beginning of the twentieth century, this scenario had changed considerably. The forces of industrialism and urbanization put great pressures on the schools to educate children for life in the modern world. Cities, overwhelmed by the population rush from the rural areas, were also overwhelmed by the vast numbers of immigrants from East-ern Europe. Community leaders called for schools to be organized on a more efficient and standardized basis, even as reformers surveyed the conditions of life in the slums with justified horror. Businessmen, impressed with the efficiency movement based on the ideas of Frederick Taylor, called for a new type of school system to do a better job of preparing workers. Similarly, psychologists, buoyed by the work of Edward Thorndike and G. Stanley Hall, felt that education could be put on a more scientific basis. Thorndike agreed with many progressives that technological expertise held the key to the future. The remedy for America's educational ills, Thorndike wrote, was for the common man to refuse to think beyond his limited field and to learn to consult the expert, whether the matter be medicine, education, or government.[9]

Though progressives generally believed in the power of technology as a means to improve the world, the term "progressivism" defies exact definition. It meant different things to different people and seemed full of contradiction and paradox. For example, the aims of religion and science can be seen as diametrically opposed; yet science and religion at times merged in the progressive era to form a powerful animating force for human betterment. While the progressive era brought a more insistent claim and reliance on formally trained and technically competent experts, the educational leaders who emerged at the beginning of the twentieth century had not abandoned totally the evangelical spirit of the common school movement. Many of the new educational leaders were sons of Protestant clergymen.[10] Edward Thorndike, Leonard Ayers, Sydney Pressey, William Kilpatrick, Paul Monroe, Lewis Terman, and Bruce Payne were among this group. Others, like Charles Judd and G. Stanley Hall, had planned to become ministers before turning to psychology. Religious as well as scientific and business metaphors were common in describing the teaching craft. Celebrating the teacher in 1898, John Dewey wrote, "The teacher is the true minister of God and the usher of the true kingdom of God."[11]

Nonetheless, a new attitude was finding its way into education. As women assumed more and more the role of subservient employees, men assumed leadership positions in the new field and made education a lifelong career. Emphasizing the scientific character of education, they attempted to rescue education from the vicissitudes of politics and from the arbitrariness of moral concerns. Education, they argued, needed a centralized leadership armed with an objective expertise. Rather than talking about the 'evils' to be scourged and overcome by the school, they talked increasingly about the 'problems' to be solved by experts.[12] This change in perspective entailed in some ways a change in progressive thinking about the place of educational institutions in a democracy. And it raised at the same time a vexing theoretical and practical problem. The concept of educator as expert seemed to hold great promise. If educational leaders became experts, then it appeared more likely that the schools could become that credible social force needed to produce a more perfect and harmonious society. Yet expertise seemed to allow an element of elitism to enter the craft. If the experts ruled, then democratic rule by the people would suffer as a result.

Historically, this dilemma was not new. When Plato and Comte had suggested rule by a knowledgeable elite, they had abandoned all pretense to democratic government as a consequence. Comte believed that citizens in a technocratic society should come to trust governmental experts in the same way that patients obey their doctor. The progressive allegiance to democratic reform made the matter more difficult. On the one hand, the progressives wanted to revitalize government by the people. On the other hand, their belief in the efficiency and effectiveness of the expert resulted in the effort to keep politics distant and to create institutional systems that would separate the people from the very processes that might most affect them. Samuel Haber points out that many times these dual efforts might be seen not only within the same social movement, but also within the same political formula and even within the same men.[13] The way these efforts were alloyed and eventually resolved in the thinking of the major leaders in the progressive movement presents an opportunity to judge the appropriateness of expertise to education. Particularly in the lives and thinking of Ellwood Patterson Cubberley and George S. Counts, we face for the first time the problems that may arise when the belief in expertise is connected with a belief in the socially and personally empowering nature of education.

Ellwood Cubberley: The Professional Elite

Ellwood Cubberley's life and career lay at the heart of the movement to create a new breed of expert educational managers. In 1898, he was offered a professorship in the Department of Education at Stanford University after brief service as a geologist and as superintendent of schools in San Diego. He was given the Stanford post with the understanding that unless the department quickly became academically respectable, it would soon be disbanded.[14] Cubberley had never had an education course, yet he had in mind a dozen courses he might teach in school administration, school problems and organization, and educational history. The available literature in the field of education was sparse, but Cubberley persevered, eventually writing his own history of education, which for many years assumed the status of educational dogma. In this work he extolled the beginning years and development of education as noble efforts to overcome the forces of industrialism, urbanization, and immigration that had engulfed and changed nineteenth-century America. He celebrated early educational leaders as "public men of large vision" who were faithful not only to their Protestant upbringing but to the demands of a society that required state-supported and -managed education.

Cubberley approached the history of education with a partisan view. He wished not only to "make the Department of Education at Stanford famous," but also to promote the idea of common schooling, small-town virtues, and the social evolution of educational progress.[15] Part of that evolution entailed the easy mingling of pietism with science. Cubberley, a trained physical scientist, found the ideal of science so compelling that the carryover to the field of education seemed natural and crucial. Even the religious objections that had so marked intellectual debate in the nineteenth century did not stand in the way. "I believe firmly in God and the Principles of the Christian religion," Cubberley once affirmed. "I am in the strongest sense a harmonizer of Religion and Science; there is no conflict in my mind between the two."[16]

Such assurance soon proved to be the mark of the man. In his first year at Stanford, Cubberley not only headed the education department but taught five courses and delivered over seventy-seven addresses. He never seemed to doubt publically his own competence despite his lack of educational training. He endeavored to make formal education required in the specialized areas he came to favor: vocational guidance, school hygiene, statistics, educational psychology, methods of teaching, and many others. By the time he had retired from Stanford in 1933, he had written sixteen books, innumerable articles, and edited one of the most influential series of books on education of his day. Through shrewd investment, he had also amassed a considerable personal fortune that enabled him to personally finance an education building on Stanford's campus. In true Jeffersonian fashion, he not only donated the money for the building, but also designed it and served as its first librarian.

Despite these remarkable achievements, Cubberley has his critics. In his study of the progressive era, Cremin gives Cubberley but a few lines, and those to criticize him for his ethnocentric views of East European immigrants.[17] Many modern historians use Cubberley, not as a definitive source, but as a way to point out how not to do historical writing.[18] Scholars reviewing his other written work have assessed that his most notable scholarly achievement was not original, but a collection of edited writings that might still serve useful to professors teaching a survey course on educational thought.[19] This appears to echo an early assessment of Cubberley's powers of scholarship made by E. L. Thorndike, who had served on the graduate committee approving Cubberley's doctoral dissertation, a document that had been written in whirlwind fashion during a span of three months. "Cubberley is a good man," Thorndike noted, "but not a good scholar."[20]

It would be wrong, however, on the basis of these assessments to dismiss the significance of Cubberley's career. If Cubberley was not original, his thought did resonate with some of the deepest currents of American opinion, and his assured sense of such opinion was enough to give it added weight and momentum. In this regard, the most notable achievement of Cubberley's distinguished career was his contribution to the creation of school administration as a specialized field and profession. This contribution was firmly grounded in faith in the expert. Cubberley was convinced, with a firmness that made believers of his students and colleagues, that education should be controlled by experts employing the latest techniques in scientific management. Not everyone could be an expert, and Cubberley promoted a rigorous selection process that required both service in the schools and extended educational training. Business provided the model by which schools could be efficiently run, and Cubberley's works abounded with metaphors connected with the world of commerce. He also pointed to the physician as that model by which the new educational professional should be publically measured. He complained that "while a good superintendent of schools takes about as good a thorough preparation for his work as does a physician or surgeon for his, and is about as competent in his professional field as is a physician or surgeon in his, the public does not understand this."[21]

According to Cubberley the public also did not always understand that in the complex world of school administration, educational affairs might best be left to the technically competent. Cubberley repeatedly criticized school board members who would sacrifice "educational efficiency for political expediency." He distrusted the practice of electing school board members through the ward system, preferring instead city-wide elections that would produce "better men" and eliminate the "inevitable representation" from the poorer wards.[22] Cubberley certainly did not want to disenfranchise the public entirely from the running of the schools, but he shared the progressive belief that in the complexity of modern industrial life, politics had little place. In his eyes, school board members were "upright citizens" who were "more or less successful in their different lines of work," but they needed to understand their role. "The chief trouble with them [school board members]," he wrote, "is not their honesty or general intelligence or their willingness to serve, but rather that they know so little about what constitutes good school administration that they are likely to think that, because they have children in the schools, they know all about how schools should be conducted."[23]

Few criticized such views at the time. The belief in the expert entailed a belief in a mode of governance that placed confidence and governmental power in a credentialed few. While this was not easily reconciled with a belief in democracy, the appeal to a curious mixture of scientific, medical, and business metaphors allowed many progressive thinkers to sidestep theoretical problems. For example, an early supporter of the importance of expertise, Nicholas Murray Butler of Columbia University, commented that it was as foolish to speak of "the democratization of the treatment of appendicitis" as to speak of "the democratization of schools.... The fundamental confusion is this: Democracy is a principle of government; the schools belong to the administration; and a democracy is as much entitled as a monarchy to have its business well done."[24]

In a similar fashion, Cubberley celebrated the democratic origins and focus of public education but argued that power ought to rest firmly in the hands of a knowledgeable elite. This allowed for a coherent conception of school administration, but it also permitted lines of argument that now appear more troublesome. For example, Cubberley praised the plurality and breadth of the American character but warned that unless "the docile, illiterate, and unmotivated immigrants from Eastern Europe were quickly assimilated they would dilute tremendously our national stock, and corrupt our city life."[25] He found school teachers notable for their commitment and practical knowledge but felt that they should not be included in the process of determining school policies. Finally, he lambasted politically based selection processes, but he worked to establish a networking system that assured good employment opportunities for his "boys," the graduate students who trained under him.[26] It is important to note that in this latter effort, Cubberley did not labor alone. He competed and collaborated with other educators also keenly interested in establishing educational administration as a field, especially George D. Strayer and Nicolaus Englehardt at Teachers College of Columbia and Charles Judd at the University of Chicago. Apparently Cubberley's influence was particularly effective. After visiting Cubberley in Palo Alto, an educator once commented that "Cubberley had an educational Tammany Hall that made the Strayer-Engelhardt Tammany Hall in New York look very weak."[27]

Cubberley was a man much celebrated and revered in his time. His biographers spend a major portion of their book detailing the many honors and recognitions given him upon his retirement. His financial success was so notable that a prominent business journal dispatched an investigator to write an article on his investment strategies. Cubberley was a loyal man, full of good will in interpersonal relationships, a man who apparently fostered such sentiments in others. Upon assuming his first superintendency, one of his graduate students wrote that "the thing which will mean most to me will be Dad Cubberley's estimate of my work. I don't care what other people say—if Dad Cubberley says I've done a good job, I'll consider myself a success."[28]

Nonetheless, it might be asked how so many of Cubberley's prejudices so noticeable to modern observers might have escaped mention at the time. David Tyack has explained that many of Cubberley's opinions simply echoed the thought of most educators of his day, becoming invisible simply by being commonplace. Also, they appeared to be supported by scientific evidence and research, research that by virtue of its claims to objectivity seemed to escape the subjective pitfalls of moral and philosophical debate. In this context, it is important to note that Cubberley never considered himself a philosopher, nor was he much interested in the social issues that dominated the thought of other progressives. Indeed, in the hundred books he edited for his series on education, not one was on a philosophical topic. As late as 1933, Cubberley did not include John Dewey in his list of the twenty most influential men in the evolution of education as a field.[29] Conversely, he found great merit in the work of such people as Lewis Terman, whose work on intelligence testing promised to make scientific the inevitable sorting process of the schools, and Franklin Bobbitt, whose work in categorizing efficient instructional practices promised to make more scientific the work of the average school teacher.

Like many progressive educational leaders, Cubberley believed that the public school represented the chief lever of social progress. For this reason alone, the concept of education as a science and educators as pedagogical experts seemed particularly appealing. This led Cubberley to regard efficiency and competency as the primary considerations when constructing a school system. For many progressives, the language of science implied that facts were distinct from values and that managers and social engineers could realize their main interest in increasing effectiveness and productivity without necessarily dealing with such social and moral matters as the morale and character of their employees. Neither in his writings on school administration nor in his position as education department chairman, did Cubberley ever seem to adopt such a detached and uncaring position toward subordinates. Nonetheless, he regarded educational problems as matters of administrative strategy and logistics rather than dilemmas that called for reflection on the moral ends of schooling. He viewed school structure hierarchically and cautioned young superintendents to act prudently lest they get too involved personally with the female teachers who would doubtless be under their care.[30] The distance between superintendents and teachers was created by the differences in their technical skills and abilities and was to be maintained in a properly functioning district by the well-differentiated and articulated duties of bureaucratic office.

By far, Cubberley's most theoretical and philosophical work appeared in 1913 under the title *The Changing Character of Education*. In this he set forth those ideas he was to follow the rest of his career. Cubberley believed that the custodial duties of the state were likely to increase as the need for more standardization and control became more apparent. "Each year," he wrote, "the child is coming to belong more and more to the state and less and less to the parent."[31] This observation reflected Cubberley's belief in the powers of efficient managers as well as an implicit distrust of the abilities of the common person to govern. Cubberley expressed no dismay in the fact that while America was founded on the idea of equality, class divisions were unavoidable and necessary.[32] This was only in keeping with the natural differences in ability to be found in individuals, differences reflected in both the practice and structure of the schools. "One bright child may easily be worth more to the national life than thousands of those of low mentality," Cubberley explained.[33] It was precisely such differences in intellectual ability that for Cubberley and many other progressives appeared to make expert rule both necessary and admirable.

The Emerging Critique

Cubberley's belief in an intellectual elite can be understood as a doctrine of government. Belief in the expert answers the question of who should rule by pointing to the advantages of technical competence and formalized training. The expert, who has benefited from these advantages, seems to be the reasonable choice for leadership, especially if the matter under consideration is technically complicated. This view, so fundamental to the view of school administration held by Cubberley and others, later found explicit political expression in the technocratic movement led by Thorstein Veblen and Harold Scott. Conceived in the 1920s and gaining some prominence and notoriety in the 1930s, the movement was based on what William E. Akins has called the "engineering myth."[34] The myth was no more than the belief in the expert as social engineer. It was conceived out of the idea that the same principles of engineering that had achieved success in the industrial world could also be used to manage social affairs. The myth had special appeal to progressives who believed that, freed from tradition, modern man could begin to consciously shape the social environment according to disinterested and rational principles. The myth also honored the increased complexity of social matters and the administrative expertise needed to manage the ever-growing bureaucracies of the twentieth century. The technocratic belief in rule by experts inevitably ran afoul of more democratic concepts of government. Yet it was able to gain credibility by tying the American faith in the powers of technology to the utopian dream of widespread abundance and leisure.

Many progressives shared this dream, and yet acceptance of the concept of expert rule was by no means uniform and unproblematic. While most educational reformers called for a new type of teacher training and for a new type of educator, they differed considerably over just what this new educator would be like. This debate rarely revolved around any specific discussion of the pluses or minuses of expertise. More common was a concern over the particular technical and moral capabilities required of the teacher and whether matters of character or matters of technical competency were more important in determining the able practitioner. From very early in the history of the profession, this type of debate had raged with the combatants usually finding some common ground in the belief that the modern teacher needed to command more public respect and authority. Yet this summit of mutual concern was reached in the progressive era by very different routes. The progressive who was allied directly with the idea of education as science could allow that teachers also needed to be upright and moral citizens. The progressive who believed in education as an artistic or moral occupation could allow that teachers still needed to receive the very best in technical training.

Differences became more difficult to resolve when progressives began to look more closely at the educator's responsibilities to the broader social order. Here the hierarchical school structure recommended by Cubberley, Strayer, and Judd was found by some to have dubious relevance to the democratic needs of the emerging pluralistic society. The question arose of how school systems might serve as models of how institutions could allow more public participation. This concern was made manifest in views on the teacher. The emphasis on the teacher as an efficient employee and an able technician in the classroom did not necessarily lead to the idea that a teacher's expertise made her a more politically and socially responsible professional. Researchers like Franklin Bobbitt and W. W. Charters followed the principles of Frederick W. Taylor in trying to identify those distinct teacher practices that marked the labor of an able teacher. They also believed that those practices were universally applicable and therefore could be inculcated in all teachers as part of a more scientific teacher education program. Yet this very view imposed on teachers a more standardized concept of proper instructional technique and tied them more dependently to the teacher educators who now professed true scientific knowledge of what worked in the classroom.[35]

In a similar fashion, the idea of the teacher as expert/specialist with particular pedagogical knowledge and training did not always lead to the view that the teacher should have more responsibility for making educationally relevant decisions in the bureaucracy of the school. As we have seen in Cubberley's view of school administration, effectiveness was best managed by a structure in which people had distinct jobs with distinct responsibilities and duties. Curricular decisions were put in the hands of the school administrator rather than the person who was to implement those decisions. The model here was drawn from business. The administrator was the manager, and the teacher was the employee. The chain of command was from the top down, and it was apparent in the view of the pioneers of school administration that administrators enjoyed their position of dominance because of their superior intellectual grasp of curricular issues. In the most drastic implication of this concept, teachers had to do little thinking themselves, they had only to employ the standardized techniques that researchers had found effective and that principals now appropriately demanded.

Some thinkers, looking across the social landscape of technological development, were disturbed by such a conception and considered the emergence of the specialist and dominance of science with a more critical eye. Most notably, both William James and John Dewey found the idea of education as science wanting. Their reluctance to endorse totally a scientifically managed conception of education could not be easily dismissed—both men had played a huge role in the progressive effort to break free from the formalistic thinking that had dominated ideas about school instruction at the turn of the century. Both men also emphasized what was a central tenet of progressivism—that men and women can rationally and reasonably act upon the world to change things for the better. Nonetheless, James, who was a teacher of Thorndike and who had established the first psychological laboratory in the United States, believed that psychology could never offer anything in the way of predictive certainty and that teachers would need to rely on their own best instincts and intuitions to practice effectively. Teaching, according to James, was an art rather than a science and, though he looked forward to the day when "genuises" and "superior men and women" worked for the schools, he also allowed that "to know psychology...is absolutely no guarantee that we shall be good teachers."[36]

Similarly, Dewey wrote that if he had to choose between considering education as a science and as an art, he would have to choose the latter.[37] Yet in typical fashion he saw no necessary conflict between the two and sought to see where they merged. Dewey conceived of science not as a decided body of facts, knowledge, and skills to be imposed uniformly on all teachers, but as a habit of mind and as a way to interact intelligently with a changing educational environment. In this way, Dewey's idea of an educational science emphasized the original and unique contributions of the practicing teacher and had nothing of the passivity associated with rule from above. Dewey cautioned that if science were prized only for its prestige value, rather than as a means of interacting intelligently with the world, then it would be destructive to the practice of teaching itself.[38]

Dewey's emphasis on the democratic nature of science as a mode of inquiry rather than as a means of dogmatically solving human problems directly confronted a fundamental difficulty of expert rule. Expert rule could conceivably work to divide the world into two groups—those with the knowledge needed to serve and those in the need of service. The docility of the latter was of special concern to those who cherished a more active and empowered citizenry. It was precisely this docility that some began to see as the mark of an implicit contradiction in expert relations. Science and technology were seen as the most powerful expressions of human freedom and activity, and yet expert service hinted at a passivity in the person being served. On the one hand, if educators could become pedagogical experts, they might better serve their students. On the other hand, if expertise ruled, the people being governed might take a less active role in educational affairs.

George S. Counts, Social Critic

The social reconstructionists were a group of educators who took such questions to heart. Their number included Harold Rugg, Jesse Newlon, Goodwin Watson, John L. Childs, William H. Kilpatrick, and Boyd Bode.[39] Vitally concerned with the role of education in the formation of a new society, these educators shared with the educational administrators the belief that schools needed to be revamped to meet the needs of a more complex, industrialized society. They differed, however, in the depth of their social concern over the economic inequalities that the industrial order had made apparent. They also differed from the administrators in their heightened sensitivity to the moral and political issues raised in determining educational policy. The educators who tended to narrow their concerns to the operation of school systems or classrooms had less patience with abstract moral and theoretical concerns and came to view the idea of an elite class of educational experts more favorably. This seemed like an unavoidable occupational duty made more critical by the tremendous pressures of constructing the institution of the school in the early twentieth century. Yet it also resulted in a view in which the school was substantially cut off from the larger social and political context and the moral and cultural questions that might underlie it. It was just these connections that the social reconstructionists, in their aim to use the school as an agent of social change, wanted to emphasize.

Leading the social reconstructionists was George S. Counts. In contrast to Cubberley, Counts made his mark as a thinker and as an educator by his interest in social causes. He is best known now for his famous essay, "Dare the School Build a New Social Order?", but he is also considered the father of comparative education, was active in the political arena, and was an early president of the American Federation of Teachers. Like Cubberley he had a long career, but unlike Cubberley it was a career more determined by the momentum of political events than a concern over the administrative details of managing a modern school system. It is important to note in this context that Counts' career was greatly affected by the Great Depression and the glaring inequalities that became even more significant as the result of it.

From early in his career, Counts had an interest in sociology and cultural studies. He entered the graduate school at the University of Chicago in 1913 after work as a high school mathematics teacher and as a high school principal. Counts' wish to study sociology at Chicago was influenced by Charles Judd, who convinced him to stay in education and investigate social issues through the study of pedagogy. Judd, like Cubberley, was one of the central figures in the creation of education as a professional field based on quantitative and scientific principles. Judd's major field was psychology, and he had been director of the psychology laboratory at Yale before being made director of the School of Education at Chicago in 1909. His appointment to the post was indicative of the national move to make education more scientific.

As Judd's student, Counts was introduced to empirical procedures using survey and quantification techniques. Later he was to adopt a more historical and cultural style of analysis. While Counts' first publications retained some of the empirical flavor of his earlier training, his later writings tried to capture complicated matters within a broader, more general sweep. This became a constant concern of many who worked with Counts because the nuance and detail of meaning needed in close historical analysis was lost in the oversimplification of his panoramic view. Charles A. Beard, a long-time friend and associate of Counts, warned him in particular to separate history from social philosophy, to make a distinction "between facts empirically established and aspirations deliberately chosen."[40]

For Counts this was not easy to do. He was very enamored of critical analysis that sought to examine the immense social changes of the modern age. This drew him to historians like H. G. Wells and to classic social commentators such as Alexis DeTocqueville. Concerned with the movement of pastoral and rural America into the industrial age, Counts was convinced that the new age required more centralized and well-managed institutional structures, which nonetheless still had to serve democratic purposes. He was particularly sensitive to the close connection of educational structures to the cultural values of the surrounding community. "The historical record," Counts wrote, "shows that education is always a function of time, place, and circumstance...it inevitably reflects...the experiences, the condition, and the hopes and fears, and aspirations of a particular people or cultural group at a particular point in history."[41] He believed that the structure of education was a matter of choice; consequently it remained within the power of a people to shape the institution that would in turn shape "with overwhelming power the character and destiny of a people."

This firm conviction placed Counts directly within the mainstream of progressive educational thought. After he left Chicago in 1916, he served in schools of education at five different colleges before beginning his long career at Teachers College of Columbia University in 1927. There Counts joined a stellar faculty that included Paul Monroe, George Strayer, I. L. Kandel, Edward Reisner, Harold Rugg, William Heard Kilpatrick, and Edward Thorndike. He was soon involved in the study of Soviet schooling and society, which apparently did much to reemphasize his belief that institutions must be consciously formed to serve democratic values and purposes.

From early in his career, Counts was a critic of schools that served simply to benefit the affluent and socially powerful. In a series of publications in the 1920s, he used some of the quantitative techniques he had learned at Chicago to detail the selective character of American high schools, the undemocratic character of secondary curriculums, and the dominant class character of boards of education.[42] In each of these critiques, Counts expressed a dissatisfaction with the view that education could simply be considered scientifically and objectively as if political and moral decisions were not a fundamental part of school decisions. In his classic study, *The Social Composition of Boards of Education*, he particularly noted that the conception of administration formed by Cubberley and others had lost sight of more fundamental purposes by so emphasizing productivity and efficiency.[43] Counts was sensitive to findings that indicated that the people who comprised school boards did not represent the working class and thus threatened to impose upon the public a particular view of the purposes and direction of education. He argued that the public could not trust its destiny to a particular sectarian view since "the whole of wisdom resides in no single class or group."[44]

The reference to wisdom referred to Counts' view that the knowledge needed to run the schools was not to be found in simple technical competence. He frequently noted the conservative nature of school systems that served the economic and social interests of the powerful while failing to take into account the complexities of an increasingly diverse and pluralistic society. This indicated that both teachers and the wider public needed to take a more active role in shaping the policy of the modern school. While the complex school systems of the twentieth century relied on administrative expertise, superintendents also needed to make full use of the talents, knowledge, and abilities of the teaching staff. "The first purpose of any policy of school administration," Counts was to later note, "should be the growth of the teacher in courage, power, and refinement."[45]

This belief in the creative powers of teachers and their place in the control and function of the school directly conflicted with the top down approach of many leaders in school administration. Counts argued that "teaching has become largely a matter of following instructions received from some official not immediately responsible for the work with children." He advocated a new kind of teacher training institution that would emphasize liberal studies, an institution where the "most profound questions of national policy" would be debated and where "attention devoted to purely technical preparation would assume extremely modest proportions." Counts never applied himself to the details of how to improve classroom practice nor to the details of how a school might involve teachers more directly in matters of policy. Rather he contented himself with the thought that if teachers were given the right type of training, "they would in all probability demand proper conditions of work."[46]

It is difficult to say how much Counts' view of the purposes of schooling and the cultural duties of teaching was swayed by his rigorous examination of Soviet society and its system of education. No doubt, like Dewey and other progressives, he was much taken by the idea of engineering a new social order. The Russian revolution seemed to offer a great opportunity for studying such an effort. For years he was the foremost authority on Russian culture, having achieved his expertise most notably through a long tour of the Soviet mainland in a Model A Ford he had shipped to Leningrad expressly for that purpose. He later joked that upon arriving at Teachers College he wished to become involved in international education, but the rest of the world had already been divided among other scholars, leaving him no choice but to study the Soviet Union. Nonetheless, Counts applied himself assiduously, soon mastering the Russian language and availing himself of everything in print about Russian culture and history. Later, friends and associates remembered him spending time every day pouring over his copy of *Pravda*, the Soviet newspaper he received from Moscow.[47]

Certainly Counts had socialistic leanings. Unlike Cubberley, he felt that any class-based society was a travesty of human potential and freedom. He believed that the economic system of the modern industrial world needed to be reoriented away from capitalism to a more collectivist organization. The choice, Counts felt, was not between capitalism and collectivism, but between a collectivism that might honor traditional American beliefs in freedom and equality and a collectivism that might end in slavery and totalitarianism. The tremendous power of technology not only made some type of integrative economy mandatory, but also mandated that schools, and teachers in particular, be forthright and intentional in teaching democratic values and attitudes.[48]

Counts argued exuberantly throughout the 1930s for his particular view of social organization. In some ways he was as dogmatic about asserting the need for a more planned and administrative order as Cubberley was for creating a special breed of educational administrators. In this regard, both men were products of their time and the widespread belief in the powers of the human spirit to shape a more harmonious social order. The strenuous nature of Counts' reconstructionist views as much as their collectivist orientation became a lasting legacy of his career. If he had a broader, more generous understanding of the active role of teachers and the wider public in shaping educational policy, he also argued bluntly that the schools should be indoctrinators of a particular set of values and beliefs.[49]

Here some of the intricate problems that specialization and expertise present for a democratic society can be found in the spirit and thought of a single educational thinker. While arguing at many points in his career that the educational system had come under the unilateral and single-minded control of business and commercial interests that might subject the young to subtle forms of propaganda and indoctrination, Counts had little trouble advocating indoctrination of his own sort. He criticized teachers for being socially unconcerned and progressives for being afraid of "the bogies of imposition and indoctrination."[50] Pointing out that many progressives who resisted the manipulative implications of imposition were nonetheless intent on inculcating "democratic sentiments," Counts advocated that educators should be more deliberate and specific about the values they wanted to impose upon the young. He regarded as foolish the sacred progressive notions of a child-centered school, of a school substantially cut off from the pressures and responsibilities of the adult world, and of a conception of education that was passive, value-neutral, and fundamentally unconcerned with the direction it should take in guiding the developing child.[51]

Throughout his career, Counts was the center of controversy and conflict. Typically, he discussed the problems of educational responsibility in the most direct and charged terms, even employing the word "indoctrination," when other terms might have been less inflammatory and when in many other writings he had used the word pejoratively to suggest the unjustified suppression of human choice and potential. Still, especially in the 1930s, he did not wish to shy away from the real moral and political issues when he saw the world at such a crisis point and when he felt the alternatives were catastrophic. It is reasonable to suggest that Counts was moved by his experience in the Soviet Union in this matter, since there he saw the fascinating spectacle of a people embarking on intentional plans to change an entire social structure. By 1932, when he wrote *Dare the School Build a New Social Order?*, Counts knew of the dark, suppressive side of such efforts. Yet he, like so many progressives, felt that if the direction of the Soviet experiment had become perverted, the idea of consciously planning for a more just and classless state was not. In this way, the responsibilities would always fall to an enlightened few who were to be the representatives of the people in constructing and ruling the new order. His thinking followed the same line as Cubberley's in suggesting the rationale for dependence on a specialized expertise—the problems of social affairs had become immense and required the direct supervision and management by the expert.

Counts' criticism of progressivism embroiled him in bitter controversy within the movement. Some educators like Harold Rugg and Jesse Newlon agreed substantially with his reconstructionist views and with the responsibilities of educators in involving themselves in social change.[52] Others, like Franklin Bobbitt, Henry W. Holmes, and even Counts' teacher, Charles Judd, focused on the lack of specificity in his writings.[53] They complained quite accurately that Counts provided no detail in describing a teacher's role in matters of politics and school policy, in describing the real administrative nature of democratic collectivism and, perhaps most critically, in describing the appropriate methodology to be employed in the classroom. These thinkers and others who championed children's rights were uncomfortable with the advocacy of willful indoctrination and with the attack on value neutrality. Their pleas for individualism and for a more scientific education merged at this point in promoting a school system that was basically secular, impartial, and morally neutral.

Counts wished to show not only the hypocrisy of such thinking by pointing out that a nonimpositional school was impossible, but also the foolishness of such thinking by indicating the likely social consequences of a society that failed to inculcate right sentiments in the young. His sensitivity to the plight of those whom the school system did not serve—minorities, women, and the poor—as well as his developing understanding of the threat of outside imperialist powers, such as the Soviet Union and Germany, only made the matter more crucial.[54] Counts shared with progressives the view that the responsibility for education was increasingly falling on the institution of the schools and within the special jurisdiction of the professionals who served it. Yet he did not believe that the schools were the only or even the primary educational agency in society.

The irony in this debate is that the critics of Counts' views on imposition were working in the name of science to promote the schools as the exclusive educational institution, and in this way to promote the rule of the expert in educational matters. Here the concepts of the child-centered school, the school cut off from political and social events, and the school run according to scientific principles all acted as a type of cloak over the real movement to make education a more restricted enterprise run by professionals who knew best. In the case of Cubberley and Judd and other educational administrators, the experts knew best how to manage the school system. In the case of Bobbitt and Charters and other educational researchers, the experts knew which methodologies worked best in the classroom. Finally, in the case of those advocating the child-centered school, the teachers knew best the special and sacred nature of the child and (ironically) how much the forced imposition of adult beliefs might injure the child's development. In any case, the responsibilities of the professional educator were justified by the appeal to science and value neutrality. The authority of the professional expert was based on objective knowledge that was not widely shared and was free from the subjective imposition of personal values.

Still, Counts failed to provide details of what the concepts of imposition, democratic collectivism, and empowered teachers actually meant. Without those details, it was possible that the imposition of democratic values might be as oppressive as the imposition of those less noble. In his later writings Counts, ever sensitive to the winds of political change, became less concerned with questions of economic equality and more concerned with civil rights and the protection of democratic processes. In some ways this represented a turn to the right, as Counts warned repeatedly about the Soviet menace to American interests. A great irony of Counts' career was that he was repeatedly labeled a fellow traveler, and yet in his years as president of the American Federation of Teachers, he led the effort to rid the union of communists. This change in political orientation, if it was a real change, adds to his failure to describe the precise political processes that might provide for a more democratic and representative school system and thus provide a brake on expert power. Counts' own career indicated how the plurality of different political voices could extend not only to different social groups but also to the changes a person might undergo in a lifetime of service. This suggested the need to describe in more detail those institutional structures that might allow the different voices to be heard.

The Progressive Dilemma

Counts was fond of describing professional educators not as politicians but as statesmen. In this way he wished to advocate a notion of professionalism which had a fundamental regard for the input of others and which went beyond self-interest to serve the democratic mission of the schools. Counts was not afraid of the advent of specialists and a more scientific and systematic expertise. He wrote that only "through the services of the expert can a democracy make full use of the advance of relevant knowledge and thus introduce into its operations the highest possible degree of rationality and sanity."[55] Still, it was unclear how institutional and social organizations might provide a structure to insure that expertise and the rule by the expert would remain within appropriate bounds.

The call for educational statesmen honored the side of the progressive movement that appealed to both Cubberley and Counts. The movement into the industrial age required a more systematic means of education run by competent professionals. The rule of science and technology seemed to promise the means for creating a more efficient and harmonious order. Yet hard questions were also raised. Could schools both ensure a concept of profession and provide an institutional structure sensitive to the social needs of the community? Counts was critical of Cubberley's answer to that question because it provided a hierarchical view of educational administration that seemed to disenfranchise different political groups and relegate teachers to positions of subservience. Viewed in this way, Counts' critique is an argument against the excesses of a presumably objective expertise that is cut off from larger questions of political and social purpose and that suggests subservience in the people it is meant to serve.

Still, Counts did not provide an alternative system. The structure of the present school system, with all its faults, is due to the administrators who concentrated so intently on the logistical matters necessary to ensure its construction. Subsequent laments on the conservative nature of that school system, as provided immediately by Counts and other progressives and later by such critics as Raymond Callahan, needed also to reflect on the tremendous pressures put on the school system in the twentieth century to educate all students for life in the modern age. As even a quick perusal of Callahan's *Education and the Cult of Efficiency* reveals, the modern school was formed under constant pressure and criticism.[56] The progressive belief in the ability of science to construct a new social order was borne not only of a wondrous faith in the miracles of technology, but also of the dynamic of an age that presented enormously difficult problems and demanded answers.

For this reason, many progressives believed in what Eliot Freidson later described as the classic model of expert relations. Here the problem/answer approach to social affairs is reflected in the personal interaction of a client with an expert professional. The client is besieged by problems that appear to be beyond personal means and that require the help of an expert for solution.[57] Within the context of that relationship, the client assumes a more passive character and becomes less capable of reciprocal relations even as he or she puts more confidence in technical competence. Meanwhile, the professional approaches the client more rationally and technically, convinced that the justification for intervention depends more on right strategy than right relationship, more on the authority of expertise than the authority of the spontaneous will to recognize need and be of service. The efficiency and objectivity that characterize many expert/client relationships tend to be too mechanical, cold, and manipulative. Yet such relationships follow closely the modern organization of services, the codification of occupational standards, and the specialization of the labor force.

The issue confronting progressives such as Counts and Cubberley was not whether professional relationships could be avoided, but whether institutions might be so framed as to avoid the heavy costs of rationalization and depersonalization. That there are disadvantages to the doctrine of efficiency and scientific progress is undoubtedly clearer to the modern critic than it was to those thinkers and activists still operating under the heady progressive winds of social construction and a scientifically managed society. Nonetheless, it became increasingly clear to some reformers that one advanced the growth of professionals under the banner of a more scientific and technical rationality only at the expense of the volunteer, the amateur, and a more democratic participation of the public at large. This was especially true in education, which at the turn of the century had been a direct concern of such 'outsiders' reformers as Theodore Roosevelt, Jacob Riis, and Walter Hines Page, but which began to close itself off from such input as the course of professionalization moved inexorably forward.[58]

Conclusion: Jane Addams

Perhaps the greatest cost of the movement toward expertise and more exclusive understandings of practice was that concepts of education that tied social and political reform to the direct participation of the community soon lost currency and effect. This was nowhere more true than in the thought and work of Jane Addams, who was perhaps the most influential of the outside reformers in education, but whose effect on educational thought ebbed as reformers became more concerned with professional standards and technique than with the practical application of social and political critique. Addams is best known today as the founder and guiding spirit of Hull House and the settlement movement, but she was also the author of thirty-three books and over 800 articles. An incisive social critic, she greatly influenced the thought of John Dewey, and worked at providing alternatives to concepts of formal education that were disconnected from the lives of the people and from their direct participation and control.[59]

It is illuminating to see how different was her conception of governance and education from that of the educational reformers who unabashedly advocated rule by the expert. In contrast to the belief in more exclusive hierarchical structures that would limit decision making to the powerful few, Addams argued that both culture and life needed to be conceived in the broadest terms. In Addams' view, the responsibility for solving social and political problems must rest with the wider public. It depended upon the ability of the public to conceive of relations in mutual and reciprocal terms. Mutuality, in her view, required that the self interest of both the professional and the regular citizen be defined in reference to collective social interests. Mutuality, she thought, was only possible insofar as culture and politics had vital meaning to all people.

For this reason, Addams was from the beginning suspicious of a concept of professional service that might injure the reciprocal relations she felt a just democratic society required. Service in her view had to be more than one way and had to represent more than "professional doing good." It had to provide opportunities for free accommodation among different individuals and groups. Settlement workers at Hull House needed to reflect on their experience not simply to bring the problems they faced under more rational scrutiny, but to understand how the middle class, by cutting itself off from the proletariat, impoverished its sense of culture and its sense of world possibility.[60] Meanwhile Addams distrusted the ability of formal education, as necessary as it was, to reach out beyond its rigid and structured environs to effectively touch upon the needs of the people and to effectively bring the advances of scholarship into conversation with the wider public. The key to effective education was to broaden its reach, to conceive of knowledge in ways that were practical, relevant, and mutually beneficial. "I am convinced," Addams wrote, "that anything we can do to widen the circle of enlightenment and self development is quite as rewarding to those who do it as to whom it is done."[61]

This conception of education differed considerably from that of both Counts and Cubberley and required a different understanding of institutional structure. Counts and Cubberley operated in a world dominated by large and growing organizational structures and by issues of society and politics conceived in terms of large, centralized institutions. This context alone suggested a world in which the management of affairs had become too complex and specialized for the generally educated person. In such a world, the advance of expertise grew naturally out of the obligation to meet particular needs and to ensure a standard, predictable quality of service.

In contrast, the environs of Hull House harkened back to an age of conviviality and unstructured spontaneity. In the description of Lawrence Cremin, the activities of Hull House tended to be experimental, pragmatic, and studiously informal.[62] Addams herself frequently noted the purposefully unsystematic character of Hull House activities and how they had to result from whatever needs its neighbors presented. This reflected not a lack of rigor, but rather a dedication to the give-

and-take of a dynamic social scene and to the very progressive idea that educational ideas ultimately had to be gleaned from life itself. The settlement movement, Addams believed, was a protest against a restricted view of education, against all those institutional and social barriers that might prevent the active engagement in community concerns. "The ideal and developed settlement," she observed, "would attempt to test human knowledge by action, and realization, quite as the complete and ideal university would concern itself with the discovery of knowledge in all its branches. The settlement stands for application as opposed to research, for emotion as opposed to abstraction, for universal interest as opposed to specialization."[63] Simple people, she noted, wanted to hear about large and vital subjects, subjects that directly touched their lives. For this reason, they frequently offered more successful courses at Hull House than the professional experts who were also recruited to teach. They responded more to vital discussions of contemporary issues than to formal lectures.

It is perhaps not surprising that such a view of education, integrated as it was by direct involvement in community life, could not last long in the increasingly fragmented and bureaucratic environs of the early twentieth century. John Dewey, who had been a member of the board of trustees of Hull House and who had once written Addams that he thought she had "taken the right way," turned to the reconstructed school and the reconstructed society as the chief levers of social change. The once-interwined fields of sociology, psychology, anthropology, and other social sciences began to be accepted as distinct university-based fields of scholarly research. Social work itself became more professionalized as social workers became university-trained and searched for ways to replace the spontaneous and philanthropic spirit of the amateur with the scientific efficacy of the professional practitioner.[64] In the emerging and prevailing conception, reformers believed that social problems were subject to rational analysis and control and that their scope and complexity were too vast to be handled by the impulse of benevolent individuals. According to one social worker, haphazard methods of help were ineffective in an "increasingly machine governed and urban civilization."[65] The key to social reform was less in charismatic leadership than in organization and executive skill.

In response, Addams felt that professionalization tended to divide reform efforts and kill reform enthusiasm. After 1900, she noticed that the young men and women who came to Hull House wanted less and less to know about working to resolve social disorder and more and more to simply investigate it.[66] She advocated the settlement as a proper corrective to the abstract nature of university scholarship and criti-

cized "the college" for making the "test of its success the mere collect-
ing and dissemination of knowledge" rather than employing secular
knowledge in the interest of more healthful relations among people.[67]
Despite these criticisms, which became more directed and focused as
the dominant view emerged and gained force, Addams became more
associated with female altruism than with sociology or political and
social theory. This was part of a general trend in which professional
sociology began to be controlled by university departments and by
journals, and the American Sociological Association became controlled
by men. In the words of Ellen Condliffe Lagemann:

> Sociology, which came increasingly to be dominated by
> men, was more and more seen as a source for insights to be
> tested and applied by "social workers," most of whom were
> women; and settings for "social work," including social set-
> tlements like Hull House, were more and more seen as
> places to which (male) university sociologists might send
> students to collect data, which the sociologists and not the
> social workers would then analyze in a university laboratory
> and elaborate into theory."[68]

As later feminists were to note, the reality of these distinctions within institutional life reflected the ideological asssumption that values
which appealed to sentiment, intuition, cooperation, and mutuality were
inferior to values that celebrated the need for control, efficiency, dominance, and order. Class affiliation, kindness, and desire to serve could no
longer be seen as equivalent to the mastery of skill and technique that
defined a profession and distinguished a professional from a layperson
or amateur.[69] In parallel fashion, the publically acknowledged goodness
of Addams reached mythic proportions even as her ideas lost influence
and wide appeal to both sexes. As one commentator put it, Addams
came to be known more for the generosity of her spirit than for the intellectual merit of her ideas, her greatness veiled by her goodness.[70]

In conclusion, the divide that thus stretched between matters of the
heart and matters of the intellect was reflected in the divide between
women and men, between social workers and sociologists, between
teachers and educational theorists and administrators. In education,
Counts had noted that educational policy was a moral and social matter
and was left to the decisions of a privileged class only at the peril of the
wider public, who had legitimate interests in the school and thus legitimate interest in how society might be shaped. Addams raised the critical point that theory disconnected from practice and community life
was sterile, patronizing, and moribund. The status distinction between

men, who directed and formed policy and theory, and the subservient women, who applied the results of such administration in the field, tended to actualize these issues. Teachers, like social workers but unlike other professions, were involved in what was almost exclusively a corporate activity. Could they form an understanding of practice that might honor an educator's special knowledge while at the same time allowing for public input and interaction? It is to a fuller examination of the teacher as a professional that we now turn.

Three

Moral Authority and Technical Competence: The Teacher as Professional

When Ralph Hartshook applied to be schoolmaster of Flat Creek, Indiana, he found that there had been no other applicants. The job was his, but on second thought he wasn't sure that he wanted it. He felt that he had landed in a 'den of wild beasts,' full of ignorant parents and muscular youths who he would no doubt have to fight and 'lick' if he was to win respect. The last schoolmaster had been beaten by Bud Means, a brawny pupil whose father, since he paid the most taxes, was allowed to run the school as he saw fit. It was he who had conducted the job interview and gauged the merit of Ralph Hartshook's skills.

> Want to be a school-master, do you? Well, what would *you* do in Flat Crick deestrick, I'd like to know.... you see, we a'n't none of your saft sort in these diggin's. It takes a *man* to boss this deestrick. Howsumdever, ef you think you kin trust your hide in Flat Crick school-house I han'n't got no 'bjection. But ef you git licked, don't come on us. Flat Crick don't pay no 'nsurance, you bet.[1]

The main character in this novel by Edward Eggleston seems a long way from the educational statesmen recommended by George Counts or from the subservient but efficient and well-trained pedagogues described by Ellwood Cubberley. One wonders whether even the mythic generosity and good will of a Jane Addams would be taxed under such conditions. Yet the description in many ways captures some of the persistent dilemmas of the teacher. Underpaid and ill-trained, devoid of the public respect normally afforded other professionals, the teacher plies his trade in environments that seem as hostile and as unwelcoming as the students whom he is supposed to teach. Discipline, administrative chores, and merely surviving the day appear to be the goals of many teachers.[2] Eggleston's early description of a nineteenth century teacher surviving by wit and pluck in the backwoods of Indiana has been followed by a mountain of literature, both creative and scholarly, seeking to describe just what a teacher does.[3] Explicit in the literature are the questions that traditionally have been asked about the teaching occupation. Just what are the skills that a teacher needs? What is the proper training for a teacher? How can you tell the good teacher from the incompetent? How does the culture of a school affect a teacher's performance? Finally, can the teacher be considered a true professional?

It is this last question that is most relevant to the social and epistemological consequences of expertise for the everyday teacher. For if the ideological differences between Cubberley and Counts ultimately revolved around an educator's wider social responsibilities, the question of professionalism ultimately revolves around the quality of a teacher's status and relationships within the everyday environment of the school. Faced with the historical lack of respect given teachers, many argue now for a more elite and selective profession based on the arcane knowledge of the expert.[4] Yet this requires a certain understanding of a teacher's practice as conducted in the morally charged institution of the school. When set against that institutional frame, the specter of expertise raises the most disturbing difficulties.

Professionalism and Expertise

In the twentieth century the push toward the professional status of teaching has closely followed the push toward more expertise. Many educators have followed the lead of medicine in attempting to define scientifically the knowledge specific to the craft. As we have seen, Cubberley's attempt to professionalize the field of school administration was conceived in part upon the belief that science could provide objective knowledge with which to run the schools. Teachers, likewise, could begin to point with pride to the new knowledge on which to base their practice. Advances in pedagogy following Pestalozzi and then Herbart gave teachers a more sound theoretical base for their instruction, even as improvements in curricular materials and the creation of courses of study helped make teaching more systematic and uniform.[5] Later, studies by W. W. Charters and Franklin Bobbitt sought to indicate the discrete elements of instruction that marked the behavior of the effective teacher.

In the movement to professionalize education, few innovations were met with more enthusiasm than the intelligence tests designed by Lewis Terman. Faced with the unenviable task of sorting vast numbers of new students into appropriate curricular tracks, educational administrators and teachers could claim that the task could now be done with scientific objectivity and technical efficiency. Originally designed to differentiate among army inductees during World War I, the intelligence tests soon became the predominant strategy by which students were differentiated in urban schools. By 1932, three fourths of 150 large cities used intelligence tests in the assignment of pupils.[6] Terman exclaimed enthusiastically that the "importance of this new psychological tool for the improvement of school administration has been recognized everywhere with a promptness which is hardly less than amazing."[7] His fervor was echoed by classroom teachers who found that they could more easily account for the achievement levels of students by assessing their intellectual differences. As one teacher commented, "Tests have thrown floods of light on problems that have hitherto baffled me. I have felt my way in darkness as to what should be done in many cases. Now I proceed with more light."[8]

The testing movement was not celebrated by everyone. George Counts and Charles Beard both thought the movement undemocratic and mean-spirited.[9] In a series of forceful and widely read articles, Walter Lippman castigated the testing idea, claiming that it was stupid and contemptible to classify anyone as uneducable.[10] John Dewey, while recognizing the merit of the tests as a classificatory device, nonetheless argued that they had reprehensible social implications. Every person had potentials that a genuine democratic education might reveal, but that a misuse of tests might deny.[11] The potential misuse of intelligence tests became an issue for such groups as the Chicago Federation of Labor, whose members argued that "the 'alleged mental levels,' representing natural ability...correspond in the most startling way to the social levels of the groups named. It is as though the relative social positions of each group are determined by an irresistible natural law."[12]

The latter objection now appears particularly insightful, given the historical research that has been done on how intelligence tests were used to explain racial differences and classify whole groups of people into inferior curricular tracks.[13] Yet testing within the schools in some way mirrored the movement in society at large for a more differentiated social structure, one marked by differences in mental abilities and subsequent differences in occupational status. Since psychologists had claimed to discover a high correlation between I.Q. scores and occupation from the intelligence testing done on Army recruits, it appeared reasonable to suggest that I.Q. separated the professionals from the working class.[14] This reaffirmed the growing idea that the elite social and economic status afforded professionals was justified more by pure intellectual ability than by character or moral worth. Professionals were beginning to define themselves more by their expert knowledge than by their attitudes of service or self-abnegation. The amateur was distinct from the expert and the craft from the profession by the reliance on a systematic and theoretical brand of knowledge understandable only to an elect few.

This concept of a profession was a long time developing. Burton Bledstein goes so far as to suggest that the attitudes and values guiding the new occupational elites constituted a culture of professionalism.[15] To be a professional meant that one could make a living from one's services by claiming exclusive jurisdiction over a special domain of knowledge. Accountants, lawyers, police officers, social workers, engineers, and now educators asserted their knowledge of a defined discipline that could not easily be obtained or comprehended by the unlicensed and untrained layperson. Tradition and common sense took a backseat. People, more free from the occupational choices of their forebears, were also less likely to rely on traditional techniques and tactics in the practice of their new vocations. Where the craftsperson might advance knowledge by trial and error, the professional saw knowledge as a scholarly activity that allowed one to penetrate beyond the confusion of immediate experience. The professional seemed to possess a more imperial command over natural and social forces, demonstrating a mystifying ability to grasp and isolate the important variables in determining the solution to any problem. He could adopt an attitude of critical scrutiny and control toward the knowledge he had received and could determine in which direction such knowledge should lead.

This, in many ways, represented a distinct change from how certain professions had formerly been viewed. The most prevalent and influential example lay not in education but in the field of medicine. Until well into the nineteenth century the doctor's affiliation with the priest and metaphysician closely rivaled his connection to the scientist.[16] Doctors were expected to be gentlemen, and their mode of dress and their behavior were prescribed by a gentlemanly code based on chivalry, dignity, and proper decorum.[17] Lacking many of the tools, medicines, and techniques we have now come to expect, the doctor relied upon the healing hand and the consoling touch as much as upon the effective palliative. Especially in the United States, which has repeatedly demonstrated what Richard Hofstadter has called a "Jacksonian dislike for the overcultivated mind," doctors failed to achieve a strict monopoly over what qualified as professional practice until well into the twentieth century. Before the germ theory established itself as a clearly superior basis for understanding health practice, conventional medicine competed with hydrotherapy, homeopathy, and even Christian Science for the public imagination. During the nineteenth century many licensing laws were repealed in order to give free movement to the many competing ideas of health care. As one state senator put the matter, "A people accustomed to governing themselves and boasting of their intelligence are impatient of restraint. They want no protection but freedom of inquiry and freedom of action." Commenting on the wisdom of such ideas, one historian of medicine commented, "Thus did the democratic American of the day declare his unalienable rights to life, liberty, and quackery."[18]

Such thinking soon changed. The fact that such words as "quack," "mountebank," and "charlatan" now so invidiously describe incompetent medical practitioners testifies to the success of the medical community in asserting a monopoly over health care. The distinctions play most tellingly on what the doctor supposedly knows and how he is trained, rather than on the kind of personal and intimate relationship he might be able to establish with the patient.[19] In the anonymous context of the hospital and under the care of specialists, the patient acquired that ability which some have seen as a mark of expert relations—the ability to put faith in the stranger.[20] Of course, credentials and other symbols of competence were engaged to help build client confidence. The credential indicated that a certain standard of intellectual achievement had been attained, as proved by completion of properly accredited training. In this way the growth of the schools, and particulary the growth of universities as places for professional training, has been an indispensable part of the professionalization process.[21]

It was only natural that teachers, seeing the success of doctors would attempt to follow their lead. There were certain similarities. Like doctors, teachers, too, had a close connection to the ministry. And like doctors and other professionals who began to achieve their modern status in the nineteenth century, the teacher found a special place to practice. The beginnings were austere. The proverbial primitive one-room schoolhouse hardly represented the dignified quarters of a working professional. Yet it did more clearly indicate that education was a specialized practice, in some ways cut off from the community by the particular activities that were reserved for a specific location. The graded school that arose in the middle of the nineteenth century from a German model further indicated teaching's differentiated status.[22] Buildings now were constructed with smaller rooms, and more teachers with a more specific academic intent were required. Responsibilities became narrowly focused, as represented in the voluntary associations of teachers that formed in the nineteenth century. The National Education Association, though its membership was unstable and its effect on school legislation appears to have been negligible, slowly began to reorganize and accommodate better the various interests of its members.[23] The Association's newly formed departments in art education, elementary education, secondary education, music instruction, and kindergarten allowed teachers to serve their immediate needs while belonging to a larger national organization.

We have previously noted some of the work of educational administrators in the professionalization effort. They worked to centralize the common school, called for more standardized schooling practices, and demanded tougher and more consistent certification requirements, which even in the face of a persistent teacher shortage helped improve the quality of teacher training. By the 1920s the normal schools, which had been the institution specifically charged with the training of teachers, were clearly being replaced by four-year colleges.[24] Educators worked diligently to systematize their understanding of effective practice. Studies of teaching had come to so dominate educational thinking in the years between 1890 and 1930 that there is even reason to doubt that the work of such thinkers as John Dewey, George Counts, and Boyde Bode was considered actual research. In *Ten Years of Educational Research*, compiled by Walter Monroe and his colleagues covering 1918–1927, 3,650 items are listed, with not one work by Dewey mentioned and just one work included about his ideas.[25] The great bulk of the work was done by administrative experts employing quantificative techniques. Raymond Callahan points out that it was just this type of accumulation of facts and figures that served to cloak the efforts of the progressive educators in the mantle of science, frame their claims to professionalism in the language of esoteric and specialized knowledge, and protect their efforts from the challenges of laypeople.[26]

And yet few would argue that the occupation of teaching ever reached the status of the more prestigious professions. One reason has already been mentioned—the increased feminization of teaching, particularly in the years immediately preceding and following the Civil War. Willard Elsbree has documented in his history *The American Teacher* the extent of this movement and some of the social and philosophical causes behind it.[27] One cause rested on the persistent notion that the teacher more than any other professional needed to be a paradigm of moral virtue. This put the teacher squarely within the power of principals, superintendents, school boards, and the surrounding community, all of whom saw the teacher as the student's window to the world, a glass that needed to be kept spotlessly clean.

Administrators aided in this perception for several reasons. First and most practically, they favored female teachers because they could pay women less for their services.[28] This allowed a more frugal educational budget at a time when the schools were particularly beset by financial problems. Second, they believed that women, because of their inherent higher moral faculties, actually made better teachers than men. They appeared to be better employees because they seemed more docile, passive, and less likely to leave the profession for a higher paying job. These latter beliefs in particular had a muting effect on the public recognition of teaching as a profession and revealed one irony in the early efforts of administrators to promote a hierarchical perception of schooling. While female teachers by their natural faculties were thought to be better teachers with easier access to the heart of the child, they were also thought to lack the intellect needed to make curricular decisions within the school. Thus, as in the case of Jane Addams, excessive virtue became a vice, the ideological barrier to serious consideration. Matters of reason, logic, and objective judgment were thought to be male virtues, while matters of sentiment, heart, and empathy were thought to be female virtues. Expertise seemed a crucial element in professional life, but it also tended to be seen as a male quality in an occupation dominated by females.[29]

Still, we need a more complete explanation of the reasons why teachers have not risen to the level of full professionals. Perhaps it lies more deeply hidden within the dynamics of teaching, within the structure of the institution where it takes place, and within the character of the relationships that frame its practice. It is important to mention that current calls for a more professionalized teaching occupation many times evoke once again the image of medicine. The famous Flexner report on medical practice in the United States is frequently cited. Published by the Carnegie Commission for the Advancement of Teaching in 1911, this report documented the research by Alexander Flexner and began a process of professional control and standardization that did much to promote doctors to their present state of prominence.[30] References to this process further hold out hope for teachers to follow the same path toward prestige and economic reward. Yet Flexner himself later wrote another report, this time on education, which called into question the possibility of it ever reaching the scholarly levels needed to support a full and distinct profession.[31] This represents in many ways the ambiguity of teaching's status and indicates that all claims to professionalism may be rhetorical unless they are based on a firmer understanding of what goes on in the lives of teachers as they attempt to practice their craft. Many researchers have now turned to further examination of classroom practice, yet the two researchers most frequently cited remain Willard Waller and Daniel Lortie. An examination of their studies reveals many of the troubling issues surrounding the concept of teacher as expert/professional.

Willard Waller: The Teacher as Human Being

One of the ironies of school teaching is its anonymous character. Although teachers are public servants who have remained persistently in the public eye, the actual character of their work, the conditions under which it takes place, and the effects those conditions have on the personality of the teacher have remained relatively hidden. The public, historically interested in the character of the teacher as an ideal moral type, has had less interest in the character of the teacher as a human being. Teachers sensitive to the criticisms of reformers and irritated by the public's tendency to view school teaching as part-time work, frequently rebut that the critic has little idea of what it is like to teach in the schools. The schools themselves, with their cellular architecture and institutional distance from adult activity, may have added to this ignorance. Teachers practice the one profession in which there is no easy access to a phone. The point seems trivial until one considers the hardships involved in making one's living among adolescents with little contact among teachers and little contact with adults in the outside world.

Remarkably, until Willard Waller published *The Sociology of Teaching* in 1932, there had been no major studies of the teaching profession.[32] Waller, himself a secondary French and Latin teacher for six years and by all accounts an exciting and dynamic college teacher, seemed the perfect person to begin the task. His father had been a superintendent of schools in several midwestern districts. There the many fights with the local school boards had sensitized the son to the tenuous and turbulent life of a professional educator. The father had also invested his son with a keen sense of industry and a deep commitment to strong moral positions. Waller's idealism, his enthusiastic interest in the lives of the people he studied, and his dramatic flair for the humorous if slightly cynical comment make it difficult to read his studies without wanting to know more about the man who wrote them.[33]

This inclination appears fitting. Waller's scholarly bent was always to write out of personal insight and observation. Yet his research was by no means lacking in rigor. He spent huge amounts of time gathering observations, reading widely, and encouraging students to write natural histories of contemporary life, some of which eventually found their way into his works. Later in his career, Waller was involved in controversies over the increasing statistical character of sociology, and he was refused appointment to the graduate faculty at Columbia University, presumably because he was thought to be uninterested in quantification.

In part this was true. From early in his career Waller had abandoned the statistical procedures of his teacher, Stuart Rice, to adopt a more qualitative approach. Waller seemed to be less dogmatic about the issue of methodology than many of his colleagues. He argued that science had its place, but the belief that science alone led to perception was as fallacious as the unthinking allegiance to the more artistic and intuitive approach he favored. Of central importance in both methodologies was not merely the gathering of data, but one's involvement and consideration of it. He wrote:

> The essence of scientific method, quite simply, is to try to see how data arrange themselves into causal configurations. Scientific problems are solved by collecting data and by 'thinking about them all the time.' We need to look at strange things until, by the appearance of known configurations, they seem familiar, and to look at familiar things until we see novel configurations which make them appear strange.[34]

In this way the emphasis fell less on the means by which data was gathered than on the ideas that the data might be able to generate. Insight rather than quantification, he argued, was the touchstone of the scientific method.

It is important to note these disputes because they place Waller within the context of a narrowing group of sociologists who were dubious about the merits of science in defining the legitimate scholarly activity of their profession. It also reflected not just upon the method behind Waller's observations, but upon their purpose and substance. From the beginning, Waller's interests lay in examining the teacher as a whole person caught up in the complex maze of social interactions that make up the school. He pictured the teacher as someone who had to come to terms with what Robert Merton later called a "role set." The expectations built around this role helped create the teacher and imposed upon him a certain sense of responsibility toward duty; they even helped prescribe a certain stereotypical type of behavior. Waller was not deterministic in this regard, nor was he a structuralist who focused resolutely on the strength of the institution and on the functions it promoted. He saw the relationship between the conforming forces of the institution and the creative forces of the individual working both ways. Still, he was always most interested in the adaptation a teacher had to make to the peculiar social situation of the school. School represented a complex culture, bound as it was by the pressures of the community, the expectations of the parents, and the responses of the students. The "social insight" into this culture separated the experienced teacher from the inexperienced and was the source of the differences in wisdom between the two. This was not so much a matter of technical expertise as of personality and character development. "If a teacher is to grow," Waller wrote, "it must be in as much social grace as in professional skill."[35]

Unfortunately, such growth was not always positive and liberating. A consistent theme in Waller's analysis is the rigid moral influence of the community on the creative life of the teacher. Some of this writing appears dated given the more anonymous and less restrictive environments in which many teachers work today. Much of the research Waller did on the school was completed in rural midwestern towns where a muscular righteousness might have been more likely to assert its strength. He describes teaching as less an occupation than a status and a position that "places one neatly in the world."[36] Teachers were expected to be paragons of virtue, exhibiting by their lack of vices a character to serve as a model for their pupils. Teachers found themselves in tenuous and ambiguous positions, both because they had to continually monitor their own behavior and because the effect of their efforts on others in and out of the classroom was so difficult to gauge. Rarely was it perfectly clear to the public whether a teacher had succeeded or failed in his work. Yet neither could it be clear to the teacher what effect he had on the surrounding community, since all spontaneous behavior appeared to cease once the teacher entered the scene. "A teacher," Waller notes, "could not know what others were like because they were not like that when the teacher was watching them."[37] The effect of such uncertainty was to throw the teacher back on himself in a kind of ambiguous and isolated situation made worse by the fact that teachers at that time had little power with which to fight an arbitrary or unfair dismissal.[38]

Of course, such situations were full of ironies and inconsistencies and small but cumulative miseries. These never seemed to escape Waller's penetrating gaze. In a delightful turn of phrase, Waller described the schools as "museums of virtue," since it was in them that teachers were to inculcate those "nearly out of print ideals" that the "majority of adults more or less frankly disavow themselves, but want others to practice."[39] The school was both isolated and given an impossible mission: that of preparing the child for the real and imperfect world and at the same time protecting the child from it. Teachers were judged by their intellectual facility but were destined to teach always one step below the level they found most intriguing and stimulating.[40] Finally, married teachers were preferred, but mores were so restrictive that there were indications that it was "not exactly good form" to go about the courtship needed to get married. The restrictive situation was worse for female teachers, whom Waller described as our "vestal virgins."[41]

The dilemmas of the teacher did not cease once the classroom door was closed. "Teaching makes the teacher," Waller noted. "Teaching is a boomerang that never fails to come back to the hand that threw it."[42] Occupational roles attract certain types of people, but just as important, occupations tend to shape the person practicing them. Waller was cognizant of the constant pressures concentrated on the teacher in daily interactions with students. Dignity and a certain social distance had to be maintained, control and discipline had to be enforced, and teaching had to be accomplished within the particular bounds set by the interests and abilities of students. Living within a universe of adolescents, teachers had to speak with deadly seriousness of examinations, grades, credits, promotions, demerits, scolding, school rituals, and making good.[43] In short, teachers had to cultivate the ability to speak with children about childish things, while at the same time keeping the position of an adult who in all cases still had to carry an adult message into children's lives. Waller was particularly sensitive to the toll such a struggle might take on the creative and intellectual capacities of the teacher, especially since the easiest and least bothersome means of practicing the craft was simply to fall into the habits and ruts already provided by the institution of the school.

Waller was never too sanguine about the possibility of teaching attracting the finest minds. The public standing of teaching, the low pay, and the lack of opportunity for advancement all seemed to mediate against such an eventuality. Some evidence suggested that the students entering teaching were not as academically gifted, and Waller cited his own observations of students gaining certification only as an "insurance policy" against the failure to find more satisfying work. Nonetheless, Waller wondered if merely raising the salary of teachers would be the real answer for attracting better people. He questioned whether we had in fact "over-rationalized" our ideas of occupational choice and whether the reasons people entered the field were more intuitive or simply more connected with the desire to escape from the "soil" of the world into the safe confines of the school.[44] Besides, he saw the effect of the culture of the school as far more important in determining excellent practice. Waller's portraits of school life conveyed the moral complexity of the institution and the strong and complex character needed to manage it.

In all of his many vignettes of classroom life, most of which came from interviews conducted by Waller or his students, the focus rests squarely on the teacher as a human being. The fact that schools were run with a monotonous regularity, that communities tended to see teachers in stereotypical ways, or that teachers themselves found it necessary to adopt certain poses as a means of interacting more effectively with students—all tended to deny the teacher as a full human character complete with adult needs, including the need to grow spiritually and intellectually. Waller was aware of the many suggestions existing even at that time that the occupation needed to become more professionalized, to adopt tougher standards for entering the craft, and to increase the amount of schooling required of the beginning teacher. He was not resolutely opposed to such ideas, but he doubted whether such efforts would necessarily lead to an increase in the social standing of the teacher. Teachers lacked prestige, he felt, because the community failed to see them as ordinary people, a fault partly caused by a narrow social and intellectual training that tended to isolate them from the rest of the community and perhaps to destroy some of their essential qualities as human beings.[45] He proposed another solution. "Perhaps what will do the teacher the most good," he wrote, "will be for him to have an opportunity to take leave of his profession, both during his training and after he has begun to practice his trade, and to mingle with his fellow men as an equal."[46]

This proposal, so opposed to the considered opinion of the time, was typical of Waller's thinking and of the enthralling nature of his personality. He was known in his classes for considering the opposite course, for attempting to see things in a contrary way, if for no other purpose than to break free of the restrictive modes of conventional thought. Students at times felt this to be a device for freeing them up and for pushing them to overcome their quiet exteriors as they became more critical and analytical thinkers. Yet it was no mere pedagogical strategy. Waller shared with his contemporary and idol, Thorstein Veblen, a disconcerting capacity to see beneath the surface of appearances, to explicate the hidden logic of ordinary poses and uncover hidden reasons for human action. He had a tendency toward iconoclastic views, toward cynicism, and even toward violent and shocking positions. Yet this indicated more than a manipulative and idiosyncratic nature; it indicated a strong moral interest. In the words of Everett Hughes, who was a classmate of Waller's at the University of Chicago, it was a mistake to confuse Waller's "sardonic detachment" for a "misanthropic attitude," since it actually revealed a "deep attachment to the human race…not to one race or breed, but to the whole species."[47]

Waller liked to consider himself a "disturber of the peace," and friends described him as "prone to challenge stuffed shirts in high places." He was an idealist who could not help but feel a sense of personal injury when men and institutions did not live up to his ideals and the world appeared different from his hopes for it. Despite the hard-hitting, dismal realism of his writings, there was a touch of romanticism in Waller, a kind of deep faith in the human potential if it could only discard the excess baggage of ego, vanity, role-playing, and institutional restraint.

Perhaps it was not surprising, then, that Waller could not believe that teaching would be reformed merely by the teacher's donning the more prestigious dress of a full professional. Such a move might yield more prestige, but at the price of further isolating the teacher from the real world and the everyday fellowship of common people. From Waller's viewpoint, a larger threat to the school was its own structure, the very tendency of an institution to become inflexible, mechanized, and dogmatic. The damaging effect this could have on the creative spirit of teachers and students was at issue. While institutions provided the necessary organizational structure to sustain an idea, they could also kill an idea by encapsulating it in the routine or by making it a habit.[48]

In Waller's view the opportunities, indeed the pressures, for both students and teachers to fall into ruts were legion. Given the responsibility to evaluate students, teachers could adopt a static, safe, mimetic, and even juvenile conception of what counted as good performance. Given the responsibility to control classes, teachers could easily confuse punishment with discipline and enforce drill and habit rather than participation. Given the responsibility to cover a package of material within a certain timeframe and within a certain social structure, teachers could fall prey to the clock and to the dull routine of recitation that rarely changed from year to year or class to class. Finally, given the responsibility to always know and "wax unenthusiastic over any subject under the sun," teachers could fall prey to a didactic attitude that made learning by teachers and students almost an impossibility.[49]

It was in this latter criticism that Waller confronted most directly the problems of expertise and rule by the expert. For if the teacher was the expert authority with the responsibility to know, it might soon become inconceivable that the teacher too had to grow, that the teacher was given to doubt and ambiguity, and that the teacher might be trying to learn as well. Waller's analysis more than once hints at the Socratic irony of teaching, at the idea that one's personal standing as a teacher was achieved by being a good learner, yet one's social status as a teacher was achieved by appearing to be full of knowledge and therefore beyond learning. The stereotype of the completely formed teacher is given great play by Waller, not only because of the unreasonable demands of the community, but also because that stereotype can be absorbed by the teacher himself. The teacher can fall prey to the pressure of a 'teacherish' domination and subordination in which one's authority is maintained by continually seeking opportunities to pour out one's great knowledge into others.[50] The conforming silence of students is one liability of fitting this stereotype. A more subtle liability is that the teacher can lose the attitude of being a learner and thereby lose the exciting possibility of learning from one's students.

Waller's final recommendations argue against teachers being considered an exclusive and elite class. Given the pressures of the school, the need to keep control and keep one's job, teachers should find great solace in one another's company. They might find strength in numbers and in the collective wall of resistance this could provide against the unreasonable demands of administrators, parents, and students. Yet as comforting and necessary as such associations might be, they also might only further separate teachers from the communion with their students and from the rest of the adult world. Waller worried that the teacher's ties to his primary group (his fellow teachers) might take precedence over his obligations to the secondary group (his students).[51] Successful teaching resulted from tearing down walls rather than building them up. Although students as well as teachers can erect walls that make learning more difficult, Waller thought that the wall of teacher domination, made more firm by an exclusive status, was doubly damaging. At its barricade fell the development of creative imagination. The schools, he argued, needed more freedom and spontaneity if the personalities of both the teacher and the student were to be developed and renewed.

It was in this latter context that Waller presented his most striking suggestions. He wondered seriously about the invigorating effect of inviting the most competent leaders of the adult community who were not teachers into repeated and meaningful contact with the young. He thought that schooling might be aided by larger numbers of people entering teaching on their way to another occupation.[52] The pool of people in this latter group had been limited by the increased standards of the profession. But Waller suggested that the vigor of these people might more than make up for their lack of training in educational technique. By these last suggestions, Waller meant no disrespect to teachers whom, despite his criticisms, he both loved and respected. Rather, as always, he wished to point out that teachers were adults too, that they needed association with other adults as well as their assistance and creative energy. Waller was aware of the importance of creating licensing requirements for a profession. They served to protect the public as well as to create the exclusiveness needed for elite status. Yet he was sensitive to the stultifying effects of an overly structured and static environment on the development of personality. In his consideration of the formalistic and bureaucratic context of the school, the screens of a more exclusive professionalism seemed only to be part of the problem.

Daniel Lortie: The Teacher as Expert/Professional

The world had undergone great changes in the time between the publication of Waller's work and the work of Dan Lortie. The United States had emerged from World War II as a dominant force in world affairs. The threat of nuclear annihilation, the pace of technical achievement, and the growing and more evident interdependence of economic markets made the world seem a far more complex place in which to live. The schools seemed to be in a constant state of crisis. Waller wrote at a time when the progressive dream of an open, child-centered environment appeared to be a real possibility. But the progressive movement had floundered upon the criticism of being too permissive, a fault that seemed particularly grievous in an environment dominated by the Cold War and an increasingly competitive international economy. Accountability had become a watch word of educational practice by the time Lortie had finished his study. Teachers, facing more pressures than ever before and responsible for meliorating more social problems, would need to be professionally accountable for providing productive and efficient service.

Accountability was a concept adopted from the world of bureaucracy.[53] Its application to schools indicated some of the changes the schools had undergone in the forty-three years since the publication of Waller's work. A major change was the great consolidation of school districts and the increasing bureaucratization of the schools. Between the 1940s and the mid-1970s, the number of school districts had decreased 80 percent from 101,000 to 16,300.[54] This centralization had resulted in a more complex administrative structure and a greatly increased number of administrative staff. The schools had adopted new specialties in teacher evaluation, curriculum coordination, and special education. The distance between the average school teacher and the leaders of a school district had dramatically increased.

This had many repercussions. One was the search for a means to ensure the adequate performance of tasks in each compartment of a burgeoning bureaucracy. John Goodlad notes that the search for accountability had roots in the public demand that professionals provide the services for which they were contracted.[55] Accountability also presupposed a particularly instrumental and scientific understanding of practice.[56] In this view, experience could be fragmented into separate components, each with certain measurable tasks. Accountability supposed that in a bureaucracy best results were obtained when each compartment of the system was held responsible to perform its obligations in a predictable, controlled, and productive manner. Experts were needed to guide this process, if only because they had a broader, more theoretical understanding of the whole system, an understanding that eclipsed the knowledge of common people.

Accountability was very much on Lortie's mind when he wrote his sociology of teaching in 1975.[57] Like Waller, he was interested in uncovering some of the common dilemmas, uncertainties, and pressures facing the school teacher. Surprisingly, many of those factors had not changed much, and Lortie frequently cites Waller approvingly for his insightful exposition of the hardships of teaching. What had changed from Lortie's perspective were the opportunities now available for the teacher to assume the status of a full professional. These opportunities needed to be examined, in Lortie's view, precisely because the pressures on schools and teachers were likely to increase in the coming years. Outside groups were likely to propose alternative educational practices and seek to pressure teachers to implement those practices in the classroom. As education became more centralized, state control of education might increase by the imposition of more uniform state standards. In each of these cases, teachers would become functionaries of outside groups unless they pressed for a more powerful education profession.[58]

It is important to note that Lortie had a particular understanding of the traits of a full profession. In earlier writings, he had argued that teaching was only a "semi-profession" since it lacked arcane knowledge and the autonomous control of classroom practice that such exclusive knowledge might bring.[59] In this Lortie reflected the thought of such sociologists as Amitai Etzioni, William J. Goode, and Harold L. Wilensky, each of whom had devised his own list of traits needed for an occupation to deserve the status of profession. Controversy in the sociology of the professions generally revolved around which traits were more important, not around whether the trait approach was the most helpful way of understanding professional development.[60] Most followed Etzioni's dictum that the "basis of professional authority was knowledge."[61] Goode would add the view that the knowledge had to be of such a type that the misuse of it would lead to the harm of the client.[62] Wilensky would add that the knowledge had to be systematically developed and protected by professional organization.[63] Lortie would posit that the knowledge had to be basically scarce, secretive, and beyond the understanding of those who might like to impinge on professional control—the public or outside school officials. Each of these theorists were influenced in different ways by an examination of the most powerful professions, medicine and law. These were the professions Lortie had studied and written about prior to turning to teaching. In many ways, it is possible to understand Lortie's account of teaching as an examination of the factors that might prevent teachers from assuming a social position comparable to that of doctors and attorneys.

It is fair to say that Lortie gives a somewhat dreary, though objective, account of a teacher's practice. His purpose was to understand the "ethos" of the occupation—the "special combination of orientations and sentiments which prevail among teachers."[64] In some ways, he conducted his study similarly to Waller's by relying on long interviews as well as statistical analysis. Yet he lacked Waller's gift of narrative and dramatic exposition, and he did not refer to personal observation. Other than collegiate teaching, it does not appear that Lortie had ever worked in the schools. It also should be said that the method of personal analysis that Waller used had long fallen into disfavor among academic sociologists, a change that may have contributed to the diminution of Waller's importance in the history of sociology.[65] At any rate, beyond his suggestions and commentary on his data, Lortie adopted a far more reserved position; gone is the Dreiser-like exposition of the ironies of school life.

Still, the ironies exist. Like Waller, Lortie uses teacher interviews and historical accounts to point out teaching's "special but shadowed" position in the family of occupations. Lortie notes the particular "assumption" operating in the schools that "citizens have the obligation and capacity to support and rule them" and adds that "one rarely hears anyone put forth an alternative ideology of authority in school affairs."[66] Although Lortie mentions that the normative demands on teachers by the surrounding community still exist, the most obvious constraints on the occupation are internal. Here is the greatest irony of all. The complaints of teachers about the indignities heaped upon the craft have to be balanced against the understanding that the sentiments and values expressed by teachers do nothing to counteract such indignities. Implicit in Lortie's account is the view that the ethos of the occupation is what most stands in the way of progress. He describes teachers as conservative, individualistic, and present-oriented. Each of these characteristics is examined so as to show how it actually hinders the professionalization of teaching.

The conservative orientation of teaching begins with eased entry into the craft.[67] Lortie notes that the profession is not highly selective, and that many people enter teaching having made the decision late in their schooling, or even after having pursued another occupation. Although Waller might have looked upon this favorably since it allowed greater connection with the many and varied strengths of the adult community, Lortie points out that the "heterogeneity of entry patterns indicates that teaching is not...standardized by selected criteria for admission." In addition, "the motivations, orientations, and interests candidates bring are not systematically assessed to eliminate those whose characteristics fail to fit a particular model."[68] In this way, teaching differs from the more exclusive occupations. Absent is the shared ordeal of having survived a rigorous training; absent as well is the sense of participation in a particular and well-developed professional subculture, complete with a common understanding of the characteristics of a good teacher.

Lortie notes, in this regard, that it is not possible to identify a single teacher personality.[69] The teachers he interviewed frequently pointed to the prevalence of inspiring teachers in their lives. Yet from those descriptions, it is impossible to select a single type of teacher who would seem to personify the ideal teacher. In Lortie's view, this all leads to a conservative orientation, since teachers lacking a strong identification with a common background are less likely to form concerted efforts to break with the past.[70] Eased entry into teaching encourages people who may have only a "limited interest in the occupational affairs of teaching." One cannot expect "people who choose teaching because it makes limited demands on their time to invest the effort needed to change either the context or the conduct of classroom teaching."[71]

The individualistic aspect of teaching likewise stands as an obstacle to change. Teacher individualism, in many ways, is connected with the "egg-crate" structure of the school and with the isolated nature of most school teaching. Waller was centrally concerned with the isolation of teaching because it separated teachers from the adult community. Lortie draws a different moral. He points out that the teachers he interviewed were loath to adopt new teaching strategies uncritically and spoke disparagingly of imitating another's practice. Teachers commonly spoke disapprovingly of the training they had received, criticized "Mickey Mouse" education courses, and complained that methods courses were too theoretical and idealistic to be of practical benefit in the classroom. The criterion for classroom success was to be judged by the individual teacher based on a "pragmatism of a highly personalized sort." This added to the prevailing view that teachers learned most by teaching, that teachers were largely self-made, and that effective practice was idiosyncratic. Despite talk about team-teaching, collegial relations were minimal. Teaching was conceived of as an individualistic rather than collective enterprise.[72]

This understanding was more consistent with an artistic than with a scientific understanding of occupational practice. Yet it operated against the idea of a shared technical culture. In Lortie's view, this had a negative effect on the development of teaching as a profession, since professional recognition presumed that the members of an occupation possessed collective knowledge not available to a layperson. When describing the qualities of a good teacher, the people Lortie interviewed consistently favored interpersonal skills over pedagogical knowledge.[73] This may have honored the highly personalized context of teaching, but it hardly pointed to a shared understanding of "commonly held, empirically derived, and rigorously grounded practices and principles of pedagogy."[74] Teachers, Lortie concluded, do not know how "to think about productivity as a collective matter." Lacking a jointly held conception of pedagogical knowledge, teachers were less likely to work together to govern and control the profession.

Of course, change would also be unlikely if teachers failed to articulate future goals and to identify just how shared ideas about the occupation might progress. Lortie found that teachers tended to be present-minded and, therefore, unconcerned with such matters.[75] In part, this was caused by the structure of a teaching career. Lortie noted the "front-loaded" character of teacher salaries in which one's initial pay is fairly high in relation to the ultimate earning potential of the occupation. Pay was also undifferentiated by grade or talent. Indeed, teaching was relatively careerless since advancement in the occupation could occur only by leaving the classroom for administrative work or another job. Female teachers talked more frequently of leaving for family reasons, while men talked more frequently of leaving due to financial pressures. In Lortie's view this subtly depreciated the importance of teaching.[76] Younger teachers did not see older teachers as models to emulate and were more likely to look to administration for the pattern of occupational advancement. Most teachers caught up in the tensions of day to day teaching worried about such mundane matters as overwhelming clerical duties, interruptions in class, and administrative and parental support. They failed to consider deeply the status of the occupation

and how it could be changed. Lortie found little concern about a teacher's limitation in ensuring predictable results and little "preoccupation
with deficiencies in the technical culture of the teaching occupation."[77]

Again, in Lortie's view, this orientation seemed directly related to
the prevailing ethos of the occupation. It was precisely this ethos that
time and again prevented the occupation from being based on expert
knowledge and what he called a "shared technical culture." He found
that people entered the craft mostly for reasons of service rather than
for money or for the advantages of work schedule. Many teachers
identified their purpose in moral ways and talked about influencing
students to be better citizens, stronger individuals, and decent, caring
human beings. Many had adopted an egalitarian sentiment that carried
the burden of trying to reach every student. Others talked about instill-
ing a love of learning.[78] As noble as such aspirations were, Lortie pointed out the difficulty in trying to attain such goals and the difficulty in
evaluation. Lacking ways to judge such affective outcomes and with
few witnesses to observe one's work, teachers continually faced the
uncertainty of not knowing whether they had done a good job. Lortie
pointed out how this could lead to frustration, anger, and lack of satisfaction.[79] In a particularly dismal summary, he described the teacher's
craft as "marked by the absence of concrete models for emulation,
unclear lines of influence, multiple and controversial criteria, ambiguity
about assessment timing, and instability in product."[80]

Expertise, in Lortie's view, was the answer to most of these problems. More systematic and relevant knowledge could aid teachers in
overcoming the endemic uncertainties of their occupation. With a
firmer, more collective and shared sense of pedagogical principles,
teachers could operate with more assurance and confidently demand
more control over educational decision making. By defining teaching in
less moral and inherently ambiguous ways, teachers might come to
favor outcomes that were more measurable and based on their arcane
knowledge. Finally, if teachers shared a more rigorous and selective
initiation process, there might be more collegiality in the profession and
a sense of mutual responsibility for regulating its practice.

The differences between this perspective and that of Waller could
hardly be greater. If Waller wanted to open the profession up to a more
pluralistic and eclectic understanding of effective practice, Lortie wanted to make the occupation more exclusive and open only to those who
have received a uniform training. While Waller wanted to eliminate the
barriers of artificial and institutional authority that separate teachers
from students and the adult community, Lortie wished to emphasize
the rare and scarce nature of teacher knowledge and, therefore,

emphasize the authoritative differences between teachers and layper-sons. Finally, while Waller emphasized, however ironically, the moral basis of a teacher's practice and the development of personality and personal relations in teaching, Lortie wished to emphasize the technical aspect of teaching. He would discount the reliance on moral precepts and human relations since they failed to provide the sense of mystery and scarcity necessary for a full profession.

Lortie believed that his view was forward-looking and progressive, especially with regard to the advancement of teachers. Remarkably, by focusing so resolutely on the ethos of teaching, his account contained hardly any mention of what actually occurred in the classroom or how relationships with students might shape a teacher's practice. He never mentioned how teaching conceived as a full profession might better serve students or the interests of the full community. He posed as a teacher advocate by pushing for a more resolute professionalism and yet came close to "blaming the victim" by indicating that the very sentiments and values of teachers also stood in the way of their own development.

In his final comments, Lortie referred once again to the issue of accountability. He noted that while teachers had begun to adopt a more "militant" posture in their dealings with teacher unions and in their demands for better pay and work conditions, those demands might also have a backlash effect. The public, viewing the teacher as someone rela-tively well-paid who wanted to be honored with more dignity and con-trol in daily practice, might also come to expect higher levels of teacher competence.[81] Here, as elsewhere, the call for teacher expertise present-ed itself as an argument against ambiguity. Teachers required expertise to eliminate the endemic uncertainties associated with their practice. The public demanded expertise to eliminate those ambiguities and pat-terns of befuddlement associated with modern social problems or with merely making one's way in a complex world. Lortie pointed out that increasingly the schools have been pinpointed as social problems them-selves. The demand for expertise arose from the possibility that the peo-ple who sought authority in the schools might not know what they were doing. For this reason, Lortie argued, teachers needed to adopt the pos-ture of a full profession and assert that they are in control.

Conclusion

As we have seen in this chapter, it is possible to view the modern quest for professionalism as an assertion of expertise. When Cubberley and others sought professional status for the field of school administration, they also sought a way to distinguish the occupation intellectually from others. Such distinction gave authority to the members of the occupation and allowed them to exert certain rights of practice in the operation of the schools. If teachers were to exert similar prerogatives in the classroom, it seemed reasonable that they too would have to gain control over a knowledge base that went beyond the understanding of the common layperson.

Both Lortie and Waller were aware of the many historical factors that might stand in the way of such an eventuality, not the least of which was the moral context and aims of the teaching practice. It was precisely this context as represented in the close ties between the community and the school that moved Waller to note the constraining influence of rigid moral belief. Waller did not wish to deny teaching's moral basis, but he did wish to show how incapacitating an artificial and overexuberant moral authority might be to the development of personality. Waller hardly mentions the technical subculture that Lortie finds so central to the development of the profession. In Waller's view, teachers and teaching practices suffer when they are isolated from the context of the real world and commerce with ordinary human beings and normal experience.

Lortie's description, couched as it is in the familiar language of modern sociology and in the language of institutional function and responsibility, seems more sophisticated than Waller's. The community has largely disappeared in his account, and what remains is the shadow and dream of professional prerogative and competence. One suspects that the influence of teaching's moral basis and purpose takes a backseat in his analysis because, in his view, moral values and beliefs lack compelling social force. His arguments for a shared technical memory are one-sided in this regard, but they were so compelling to the many reviewers of his book that hardly anyone questioned just what he meant by the term.[82] Thus, Lortie could call for more collegiality on the basis of technical competence and yet not feel compelled to indicate just what such competence might entail. His argument seemed totally in keeping with the most recent conceptions of professional authority.

This point seems important to press for several reasons. First, it is not easy to specify the technical content of a teacher's expertise. Joseph Featherstone, the one reviewer who sought to analyze Lortie's book in the historical context of Waller's work, notes that the profession of teaching is "so complex and our modes of knowing about it so limited, that it is difficult to believe that any emerging paradigms of technical knowledge will be anything but scientistic mumbo jumbo."[83] Several years earlier, Philip Jackson's account of school teaching, *Life in Classrooms,* had reached much the same conclusion. Noting the disparity between learning theory and teaching practice, Jackson had argued that technological conceptions of teaching were simplistic and failed to account for the many contingencies that prevailed in classroom experience.[84] His observations of teaching had convinced him that teaching was such an opportunistic and unpredictable process that any scientific or technical conception of the craft was likely to be limited and mechanical. A more artistic and intuitive sense of the craft could not be discounted. Given the complexity of his work, the teacher must learn to tolerate "a high degree of uncertainty and ambiguity. He must be content with doing not what he *knows* is right, but what he *thinks* or *feels* is the most appropriate action in a particular situation. In short, he must play it by ear."[85]

The positions of Jackson and Featherstone suggest that Lortie's analysis may be ideological. Jackson holds that it would be silly to discount the impact of science on teaching, but it would be equally silly to suggest that scientific conceptions can account for the give-and-take, the ambiguities, and the vicissitudes of classroom experience. Lortie wishes that the profession would impose a more standardized understanding of a common type of teacher. He suggests that teachers should adopt the special esoteric language of experts as a mark of their arcane knowledge. He recommends that teachers adopt a collegiality that might determine the perimeters of effective and recommended practice. One can sympathize with these positions precisely because of the many pressures on teachers and the lack of collegiality and interest they exhibit toward understanding the principles underlying their work. Yet one can also understand Waller's view that standardization has its dark side, and that one puts on the straitjacket of social conformity at the risk of sacrificing the zest and creativity that make good teaching a vital act. Given the public nature of a teacher's practice (teachers are unusual in that they have to practice their occupation in a crowd), it seems just as reasonable to suggest that the lack of special language is an asset rather than a liability. At the very least, the idea of imposing what David Tyack has called the "one best system" on admission practices seems premature and self-serving, since there is little universal agreement on what counts as good teaching.

One cannot help but note in this matter how little Lortie listened to and approved of the comments of the people he interviewed. They pointed consistently to the importance of human relations in teaching and the importance of teaching's moral consequences. Notable by its omission from Lortie's catalogue of characteristics is the trait of service, which perhaps most defines a profession. While the sincerity of this trait has recently been questioned by certain radical commentators, many early sociologists saw it as a main aspect of the professional character.[86] The attitude of service indicated that one practiced for the benefit of others rather than for personal gain. This separated professionals from other workers and indicated that in some ways they had escaped the excesses of a materialistic and capitalistic culture that sought to evaluate every act according to the harsh tests of least cost and most efficiency. As ambiguous as the element of service might be and as uncertain as moral rewards might be, it was these characteristics that came across the strongest in the people Lortie interviewed.

Finally, it must be said that the very nature of professions has come under intense scrutiny since Lortie wrote his work. While recent proposals for making teaching more selective have followed many of Lortie's suggestions, some commentators on schooling have raised the issue of whether the idea of a professional expert might not be wholly inappropriate to a teacher's trade. This tradition has a long history of looking at professional practice in a more critical light, of questioning the credibility of scientific expertise, and of viewing the professionalization process as a political strategy. A fuller understanding of expertise and education will need to make some note of this tradition.

Four

The Teacher as Expert Authority:
The Romantic Critique

Daniel Lortie's vision of a more exclusive teaching profession responded in part to a group of educators and social critics who emerged in the
1960s and 1970s and took the limits of expert authority and competence most to heart. The critics were called romantics because of their
ideological ties to Jean Jacques Rousseau and his belief in the natural
goodness of humans and the perverting influence of artificial institutions. The romantics included, among others, Paul Goodman,
Jonathan Kozol, Herbert Kohl, John Holt, Edgar Z. Freidenberg, and
Ivan Illich. Many of the romantics were teachers or former teachers,
and many had taught disadvantaged students. They shared in this way
a personal sense of outrage over the lack of educational opportunities
provided to large segments of the population. They also shared a disdain for modern industrial life which they considered racist, repressive,
and overly mechanized. The school, in their view, was a conservative
institution. To support the school meant to support a system that per-
petuated the power of the elite classes.

To understand the romantics fully, it is necessary to place them in
proper historical perspective. The modern critics, like many romantics
of the past, saw themselves as rebels. Such is the disposition of a movement that would place individual development and the primacy of emotional and subjective expression above all rationalized systems and
beyond all traditions. Yet it reveals an intrinsic arrogance. The modern
romantics did not suddenly, like Athena, appear full blown upon the
educational scene. They descended from a long line of political and literary thinkers stretching from Jefferson and Jackson to the modern
populists, from Thoreau and Emerson to Henry Miller and Kurt Von-

negut. Jack Williams has pointed out that the modern romantics had ties to the American tradition of rugged individualism.[1] This tradition celebrated values such as self-sufficiency and independence, stressing the equal competence of the common human being. While such beliefs have frequently resulted in strains of anti-intellectualism in the American character, they also have prevailed as the vital elements of an enduring belief in the frontier spirit and in the immediate utilitarian motive.[2] In the best sense they were part and parcel of the democratic belief that no special group should mediate between the truth and the common person.

The romantics also were part of a tradition of thinkers who looked dubiously and even fearfully on the effects of industrial and technical development upon the American scene. Thomas Jefferson's belief in an universal education system was based not just on political analysis — the need for an educated electorate in a republic — but also on the belief that yeoman farmers were "the chosen people of God."[3] Jefferson believed, with many others, that direct contact with nature yielded industriousness and freedom, while involvement in manufacture and commerce yielded dependence and subservience. Jefferson presaged what would become a motif in anti-technological literature, namely that technology perverted or discarded a more organic understanding of a human's relationship with nature and undercut the vital basis of human morality.[4] Later, when Emerson and Thoreau looked upon the changing American countryside dotted by factories and dissected by road and rail, they wondered whether "we ride the railroad or the railroad rides us." Their fear of and disdain for the restrictive order of technical development was part of their romantic belief that science and objective rationality failed as a means of comprehending reality.[5] By ignoring the poetic, emotional, and nonquantifiable dimensions of life, science might begin to constrain the human imagination in systems just as destructive of the organic nature of the human psyche as of the natural environment.

The argument against technology revealed the love of the romantics for unviolated nature. Romantics have traditionally stressed the need for self-discovery, believing life's pure and simple beauty should unfold naturally, unimpeded by the artificial and impositional forces of civilization. They have honored that which is unpredictable and spontaneous rather than that which is systematic and controlled. "Whoso would be a man, must be a nonconformist," Emerson wrote.[6] For this reason romantics distrusted formalized educational systems, believing them to be damaging to the natural development of human beings and their need to explore a personal understanding of the world. Romantics complained that school systems too often sacrifice the personal nature of learning for the need to adequately train students in the manners, morals, and knowledge suited to particular institutions and traditions.

Nonetheless, romantics did find their way into schools and into discussions over educational theory. Hofstadter points out that in setting up a potential conflict between the needs of the child and the imperatives of the social order, child-centered progressives at the turn of the century were implicitly romantic.[7] Likewise, Waller displayed romantic leanings by pitting the development of the individual personality against the molding influences of the institution. Modern romantics, like their predecessors, saw a great conflict between the individual and society. The conflict in the 1960s and 1970s was a key to understanding the 'generation gap' and the youth movement, a movement whose advocacy of a 'counterculture' lay directly in the romantic tradition. In the schools, the romantic movement led to an increasing concern over the primacy of student interest and to concerns over choice and relevancy in the curriculum.

On the larger social front, the modern romantic movement led to an increasing dissatisfaction with the rational, organized, and formal character of contemporary society. Theodore Roszak identified the counterculture as a struggle against "technocratic totalitarianism."[8] The revolt against planning and order became one facet of the romantic's celebration of personal awareness. The spontaneous and playful character of much of the youth culture contrasted starkly with the imperatives for efficiency, coordination, and rationalization in industrial life. Experts became one focus of youthful alienation since in Roszak's words, "in a technocracy everything aspires to become purely technical, the subject of professional attention."[9] Experts, especially since they were connected to what many youths believed to be the misguided policies of the Kennedy, Johnson, and Nixon administrations, became symbols of the evils connected with cold, dispassionate rationality. In the personage of Robert McNamara, such images were frightening; in the personage of Spiro Agnew, they were merely laughable. More generally, the expert emerged as the modern authoritarian who, because of his possession of the 'facts,' stood in the way of the truth of emotional expression. The expert was the inhibited man in the gray flannel suit, living the disconnected and ultimately unsatisfied life in suburban America.

This stereotypical picture might have been harmless and even pathetic if the more serious romantic thinkers did not come to identify the expert as a real source of power and influence. Indeed, as a brief examination of the ideas of some of the major thinkers of the romantic movement reveals, expertise came to be seen as another means by

which professionals might assert the dominance of a technical rationality. This had, according to the romantics, a particularly negative impact
on the schools, where students were molded and shaped for their slots
in a prejudiced society. The process seemed doubly unjust; it worked
socially to protect the interests and status of the professionals even as it
worked to fit others into social positions much less affluent and much
less powerful.

Paul Goodman and Edgar Friedenberg

Paul Goodman could be considered the spiritual father of the modern
romantic critics. Goodman, a poet and an anarchist, wrote on a variety
of political, social, and civic topics, but some of his most notable work
was on the nature of adolescence and on the condition of the schools.[10]
Like any anarchist, he prized freedom more than social organization.
His fondness for decentralized governmental and institutional structures grew naturally out of his critiques of the modern bureaucracy. In
his view, one of the most inefficient and dehumanizing bureaucracies
was the public school. He disparagingly referred to education officials
as "school monks." He lampooned the unimaginative character of educators who had so much control over schooling but lacked any creative
or intelligent sense about the varied needs of youths growing up in the
modern industrialized society.[11]

Goodman was a sophisticated thinker, well-grounded in philosophy and the social sciences. He frequently identified himself as an Aristotelian.[12] By this he pointed to his belief in the existence of a basic and
knowable human nature that is brought to fruition by the entire social
community, the polis. Education was a social concern, the concern of
the wider adult community, not the province for a special expert group
with a monopoly over certain credentials and skills. Yet society had lost
its intelligibility. Schools were part of a social system that thwarted the
best and most courageous aspects of human life. It made growing up
impossible.

> Our abundant society is at present simply deficient in many
> of the most elementary objective opportunities and worth-
> while goals that could make growing up possible. It is lack-
> ing in enough man's work. It is lacking in honest public
> speech, and people are not taken seriously. It is lacking in
> the opportunity to be useful. It thwarts aptitude and creates
> stupidity. It corrupts ingenuous patriotism. It corrupts the

fine arts. It shackles science. It dampens animal ardor. It discourages the religious convictions of Justification and Vocation and it dims the sense that there is a Creation. It has no Honor. It has no Community.[13]

Goodman shared John Dewey's belief in the need for all of life to be educational, but without Dewey's fundamental and positive faith in life's possibilities. He also did not share Dewey's belief in the ability of the school to make learning meaningful by forming more lively, intimate connections with the everyday social world. Goodman believed that "on the whole education must be voluntary rather then compulsory because no growth to freedom occurs except by intrinsic motivation."[14] This led him to oppose the rigid and doctrinaire character of schools, which he felt denied the spontaneous disposition and intelligence of youth. It led him to see the intervention of the schools and teachers as impositional. He wrote that the "school system as a whole, with its increasingly set curriculum, stricter grading, incredible amounts of testing, is already a vast machine to shape acceptable responses."[15]

Not surprisingly, Goodman opposed any education that did not directly serve the child's search for identity and a sense of vocation. He opposed the technical innovations that some educators had seized upon as assertions of their expert authority and technical control. Programmed instruction, for example, had recently grown out of the work of B. F. Skinner. It promised to take the guesswork out of instruction by delivering a proven curriculum that produced measurable and observable results. Following the principles of operant conditioning, programmed instruction depended on the student's use of a machine which, by small successive steps and immediate reward, delivered the learner to the desired educational end. For the supporters of programmed instruction, the method promised to make education a real science by bringing actual consistency and control to classroom behavior.[16]

In Goodman's view, programmed instruction simply closed "the window [of schools] a little tighter" and rigidified "the present departmentalization and dogma."[17] He agreed that programmed instruction might be beneficial for remedial students who had lost all confidence, but for others it was simply restricting. It was fundamentally lacking in the idea that "a student would if possible strike out on an unknown path."[18] Programmed instruction also typlified the worst confusion about the ends and means of education, since it tended to prescribe learning to the level most amenable to expert control. This involved a type of reductionism, "erroneously reducing the concept of animals and human beings in order to make them machine operable."[19] Gone was any sense of intrinsic motivation, emotional appeal, or inward intellect that might promote free and contrary thinking.

In Goodman's view, programmed instruction simply took the conforming tendencies of the school another step. It seemed inconsistent with the democratic aims of education, since it tended to deny personal responsibility. This implied a criticism of expertise, if expertise indicated an unreasonable dependence on the thinking and knowledge of others. Goodman ironically noted that after years of squelching spontaneous behavior and training for docility, suddenly upon commencement we expect students to show great reserves of initiative, to find jobs, to select a life companion, to undertake original artistic and scientific projects and to vote for public officers.[20] Goodman advocated increased educational support, but not support to the public schools, which he felt were too bureaucratic and authoritarian to do the job properly.

This line of reasoning increasingly led Goodman, and in turn other romantic critics, to reject the school as the only place of learning and the teacher as the legitimate educational authority. Edgar Z. Friedenberg followed Goodman in pointing out the absurdity of growing up in America. In *The Vanishing Adolescent,* he defined adolescence not just as a physical process, but also as a social process that led to "clear and stable self-identification."[21] Implicit in this definition was Friedenberg's belief in the sanctity of individual experience and search for meaning. More explicit was Friedenberg's belief that adolescence embodied the conflict between the individual and society.[22] Friedenberg did not mean that youth needed to be a state of perpetual revolt against society; he meant that society had to set those secure cultural expectations against which youths might measure themselves and come to a more confident understanding of who they were.

Henry J. Perkinson points out that Friedenberg was more a disciple of Rousseau than an Aristotelian like Goodman.[23] The point is important. Goodman believed that schools prevented students from coming to understand the nature of things; they provided obstacles to students' learning the truth about the world and their place in it. For this reason, Goodman favored decentralizing education in storefront stores, in small alternative settings, in order for the students to come in closer contact with reality. Friedenberg, on the other hand, felt that meaning rather than truth was at issue. The schools failed, in his analysis, because they did not seek to help students in their search for personal meaning, rather they sought to inculcate "pliability to the demands and expectations of other persons."[24] He felt the pedagogical experts in the schools failed not necessarily because they lorded over students with a punitive and overbearing authority, but rather because they treated students as "problems in social integration."[25]

The school's bland nature and its concentration on social adjustment revealed its lack of basic respect for individuality and human dignity. The solution, according to Friedenberg, was not just one type of school, but rather smaller, more diverse schools, "each serving a specialized rather than mass clientele."[26] He felt that children in this way could go to schools that were relevant to their own subjective being and their search for personal clarity and commitment.

Friedenberg and Goodman penned their descriptions about the perils of adolescence in a modern technological society in the late 1950s and early 1960s. This type of critique gained momentum throughout the 1960s and early 1970s in the youth culture movement, in the concern over civil rights, and in the demonstrations against the Viet Nam War. Friedenberg's Rousseauistic view, which emphasized the search for meaning over the search for truth, gained increasing credibility. Yet Goodman appeared to be better known. The romantic critics who followed were mainly educators who taught in urban schools and found the experience to be representative of the constraining conditions Goodman and Friedenberg had described.

Jonathan Kozol, Herbert Kohl, and John Holt

When Jonathan Kozol and Herbert Kohl were undergraduate roommates at Harvard, they probably never expected that they would become critics of the schools and writers of some of the most searching and poignant education books of the day. Kozol found himself teaching in the Boston Public Schools during the academic year, 1963–64. A truly gripping account of that year is found in his book *Death at an Early Age: The Destruction of the Hearts and Minds of Negro Children in the Boston Public Schools.*[27] Kozol had had no teacher training and was hired for only a year as part of a program to stave off integration by upgrading segregated schools. The school he described was mired in bureaucracy and punctuated by blatant acts of racism. His book stands as a type of personal testament against an educational system that stood in the way of the aspirations of its students. Far from learning from expert practitioners in the classroom, he felt that he had to unlearn many of the destructive sentiments and practices he observed in the day-to-day operation of the school.[28] Like many romantics, he believed that reform of the school was not possible, since it was constructed to serve an unjust society.

Kozol's friend, Herbert Kohl, taught in Harlem and like Kozol turned notes and papers he had gathered during the year into a stunning book.[29] Much of his book is filled with the truly remarkable writings of his students. The rest is a description of Kohl's attempts to get through the year in ways he felt honored the creativity, intelligence, and intrinsic good will of his class. The type of lesson planning and preparation techniques he had learned at Teachers College, Columbia, he found of little use. In the vagaries of the classroom, the notion of expertise as constructed out of a rational system of planning and control did not work.

> I had to react intuitively and immediately, as anyone in a classroom must. There is never time to plot every tactic. A child's responses are unpredictable, those of groups of children even more so, unless through being brutalized and bullied they are made predictable. When a teacher claims he knows exactly what will happen in his class, exactly how the children will behave and function, he is either lying or brutal.[30]

Kohl's students, like so many students today, continually faced problems of crime, drug abuse, and broken homes. This made education a daily adventure. Nonetheless, Kohl did not believe that the teacher could make excuses for the failure of a student to learn. To the contrary, he felt that the teacher needed to find "the right words or the right thing to teach," rather than believing that all learning problems "lie in the heart of the child."[31] The refusal to make excuses put the teacher under tremendous pressure, especially if, as Kohl would have it, no preselected or systematic techniques would work every day to serve student needs. The emphasis necessarily begins to fall on the dimensions of a teacher's character and strength of commitment rather than on his expert technical skill. Foremost, a teacher had to be honest about mistakes and weaknesses:

> he must be able to say that he is wrong or sorry, that he hadn't anticipated the results of his remark and regretted them or hadn't understood what a child meant. It is the teacher's struggle to be moral that excites his pupils; it is honesty not rightness that moves children.[32]

Teachers had to control their fear that if they acted honestly, the class would get out of hand. She had to observe the effect she was having on the class and act accordingly. Rather than leading the class, the teacher had to be able to be led by the class as she gauged their

response. "I have found," Kohl wrote, "one of the most valuable qualities a teacher can have is the ability to perceive and build upon the needs
of his pupils' struggle to articulate through their every reaction."[33] This
meant that the teacher, far from possessing the answers beforehand,
needed to be constantly in the act of learning. This took incredible energy and integrity, since even the students were far more comfortable with
the routine of mindless exercises and dull and secure homework assign-
ments. Instructional planning in Kohl's view did not mean keeping
ahead of the student; it meant being engaged and excited about learning
oneself. "How can the children be expected to be alert, curious and
excited," he inquired, "when the teacher is so often bored?"[34]

John Holt agreed with Kohl that the teacher is ultimately responsible in the classroom. "The idea that any nice, sympathetic woman can
without further thought, teach children to 'understand' arithmetic is
just plain foolish," he wrote.[35] He was later to note that it was just as
foolish to believe that a teacher with a Ph.D. in mathematics should be
able to teach. What were the qualities that a teacher needed?[36] Like
Kohl's, Holt's writings reveal qualities that seem inconsistent with the
idea that the teacher needs to be the dominant expert authority.

According to Holt, teacher dominance of any type has many draw-
backs. It stands in the way of the natural independence, intelligence,
and creativity of the child. Holt firmly expressed the Rousseauistic
belief in the innate goodness of the human character. "Human beings
are born intelligent," he wrote. "We are by nature question-asking,
answer-making, problem-solving animals, and we are *extremely* good at
it, above all when we are little."[37] These qualities become stunted when
teachers are obsessed with the need to have the answers and to pass on
their knowledge to children. Children learn to play the game of "guess
what is on the teacher's mind."[38] The focus in the learning situation is
on the teacher when it should be on the student. Holt insightfully notes
that even student teachers fall into this trap when they observe the
class of their expert mentor. They watch the teacher rather than the
students and thereby lose the crucial opportunity to see how students
are acting and reacting in the classroom environment.[39]

The dominant teacher might also begin to believe that learning
comes only as a result of her teaching. It is possible to fall into the
belief that all teaching produces learning. This might encourage the
teacher to always focus on her performance, rather than asking what
things are being done that hinder or help learning. Ironically, this may
be even more of a trap for the highly innovative teacher who is so full
of clever teaching ideas that she cannot wait to try them on the class.
Holt notes that "the inventors of clever teaching ideas tend to think

that if one good teaching idea helps to make learning happen, a hundred good ideas will make a hundred times as much learning happen."[40]
Actually, the learning ideas could prevent learning since they impose
themselves unnaturally upon the classroom situation. Holt tells of a
time when he had come up with a new way of teaching a class, but
soon found that the idea had taken over.

> Instead of a forty year old human being in a room full of
> ten-year old human beings I was now a scientist in a room
> full of laboratory animals. I was no longer in the class to
> talk about things that interested me, or them, or enjoy what
> I and they were doing, but to try something out on them.[41]

The teacher, instead of being so protective and self-centered, should
trust the students more and be confident enough to treat classroom challenges as opportunities to learn rather than threats to authority or personal worth. Holt began teaching at the age of thirty, and he prized his
experience since it taught him not to be afraid of the world. Like Waller,
Kohl, and Kozol, Holt speaks about the fear he found in the school.
Teachers feared losing control, and students feared getting the wrong
answer. Fear caused dependence. For Kozol, Kohl, and Holt, this
revealed the ultimate trouble with the idea of the teacher as expert
authority. The student began to depend on the teacher for the answer. In
one of his most insightful passages, Holt talks about a student whose
dependence and fear had reached such a point that she deliberately said
the wrong answer. She knew that to be correct and personally knowledgeable entailed a risk. It was much easier to be wrong and constantly
bewildered, always depending on the teacher for guidance.[42]

Ivan Illich and Deschooling

Ivan Illich took the thought of the romantic critics to its logical limits. He was at once the most apocalyptic and impractical of the romantic
critics, yet was also the most penetrating. Unlike the other thinkers, he
was not a teacher. A former Roman Catholic priest, Illich had resigned
his priestly office in protest over what he thought to be the authoritarian
and dogmatic policies of the Church. He had served as a priest in poor
sections of New York City and had done Church work in Puerto Rico
and Cuernavaca, Mexico. In both places, Illich believed that the church
adopted policies primarily to increase the dependence of the poor upon
Church authorities. Some of Illich's early writings against the Church
carry a Protestant sound to them. He dismissed the notion that the

priest should stand as the intermediary between someone and their god.[43]

This anti-clerical position could easily be applied to the school. In his book, *Deschooling Society,* Illich advances the idea that the teacher also should not stand between the child and learning.[44] Likewise, the school should not stand between the young and the more organic educational opportunities of the wider adult world. Illich thought that the school, like the church, was an institution designed to preserve the authority of the officials in charge.[45] He argued vehemently that schools should be abolished and teaching deprofessionalized. These startling ideas were actually the logical conclusion of romantic ideas about the natural goodness of the child taken to their extreme. Like Goodman and Friedenberg, Illich believed the school to be an ill-fitted institution for introducing children into the modern world.[46] Like Kozol, Kohl, and Holt, he believed that schools unfairly discriminated against the poor, and were run in an authoritarian manner. Illich's contribution was to understand these critiques in light of a wider social criticism. In his view, schools represented one element of a technological and ordered world in which opportunities had been curtailed through a new type of institutionalized poverty. The solution was to get rid of the present system and begin with something more in keeping with human agency and dignity.[47]

Illich's work, even more than the other romantic critics, can easily be seen as a critique against the excesses of expertise. *Deschooling Society* was only one of a number of books Illich was to write criticizing the "disabling professions."[48] In Illich's view, professionals adopt licensing and credentialing standards in order to protect their best interests. As schooling requirements become stricter, the knowledge over which professionals have control becomes artifically scarce. The price of schooling, as well as the artificial barriers of institutional evaluations. and prepackaged curriculums, makes it difficult for many people to become licensed. Others learn to depend on experts, since schools have taught them to depend on the help of others rather than being self-reliant. Illich calls institutionalized poverty that type of poverty effected by a credentialled and schooled society. Especially in poor countries and among the impoverished, people learn to judge one's wealth and competence by the number of years in school, even though for them extended schooling is not a feasible economic or social possibility.[49]

Part of Illich's critique against expertise is bound up in debunking the ability of educational experts to adequately and efficiently train students.[50] Most learning, Illich points out, occurs outside of school. In school, students are forced to take courses that may have little relevance to their needs. Illich points out that much of what students learn is negative, part of a "hidden curriculum" that teaches students patient reliance on a credentialled class of experts. Schools teach students that learning takes place only at one time, in one place, in the care of a special person. They teach that learning is a dull, passive affair organized in curricular patterns already prescribed by school officials. Finally, they teach that the young are a separate group who must be excluded from the varied activities of adult life. In the worst sense, childhood comes to be regarded as a type of affliction to be mediated and treated by compulsory education.[51]

Despite his call for the end of public schooling, Illich is not a total anarchist. He is not against all institutions and all technology, and he is not against a firm sense of craft grounded in the everyday reality and events of individual lives. Jack Williams quite rightly points out that even Illich found formalized education so necessary to modern life that his proposals for alternative educational institutions tend to replace one system with another.[52] Plainly, Illich argues against the immense bureaucratic structures of the schools, and against the idea that credentials can replace competence as an element of social legitimacy. Too often, Illich argues, professions define the problem so that it becomes amenable only to their service. He offers as an example the instance of the medical profession taking over the duties of the traditonal midwife, thereby transforming birth into a clinical event complete with the need for doctors, specialized medicines and procedures, and hospitals. By this transference, not only do doctors acquire more power, but also expectations of treatment are raised so as to make births without medical treatment an abnormality.[53] The same process can take place in education. When schooling credentials become required, then the schools can protect their position of dominance and authority.

Illich's solution to technological subservience is the creation of new types of education systems. In place of more schooling, Illich calls for an end to all formalized instruction that takes place without the consent of the learner. In place of more stringent controls to make teaching more of an exclusive and prestigious profession, he proposes "learning webs" that would allow anyone qualified with a skill to teach it to anyone who might want to learn. At one point, Illich recommends operating learning centers like skill cooperatives. People would be able to use educational vouchers to purchase the learning they most need. In all of his suggestions, Illich's major concern is access.[54] He wants to destroy the monopoly of the school on the goods and services of education so that more people might benefit. Illich argues that schools have control over the tools of learning—the laboratories, the machines, the equipment on which and in which people might practice their skills. For this reason, he suggests that some incentives be given to businesses and industries to open their shops and factories to those students who might one day become their employees.[55]

Illich's final chapter in *Deschooling Society* gives a more philosophical and metaphorical account of the evils of expertise. He describes two mythical creatures, Prometheus and Epimetheus, whose characters he believes match the possibilities now open to humankind. Prometheus represents the search for order, control, and predictability associated with technocratic thinking. Illich argues that this worldview leads to increased expectations built upon technical innovation. However, technical abundance is a trap that leads to physical pollution and degradation and psychological servitude. In contrast, the Epimethian character suggests a life in balance with natural need. In the place of a life built around expectation and probability, there is a life built around hope and possibility. The Epimethian world suggests a faith in human goodness, a faith in people, not products. In such a world, Illich hopes human needs would not be artificially turned into technical problems, and human wants would not be turned into commodities.[56]

Conclusion

Taken together, the romantic critics offered a thoroughgoing analysis of the idea of teacher as expert. Honoring the learning capacity and competence of the individual, the romantics rankled against suggestions of control by a knowledgeable elite. Sensitive to the limitations of a technical worldview, the romantics celebrated the emotional, moral, and nonquantifiable side of life. Romantics like Paul Goodman and Edgar Z. Friedenberg believed that schools had stopped serving the interests of the adolescent, failing to honor their intrinsic need for self-fulfillment and vocation. While Goodman and Friedenberg did not maintain identical positions in this regard, both argued against the idea of the school as the sole repository of educational authority. Both believed there was more than one way to educate and more than one type of educator. No special group should presume to claim sole jurisdiction over the type of pedagogical knowledge needed to teach.

The criticisms of Jonathan Kozol, Herbert Kohl, and John Holt were notable by examining the limits of educational authority in the classroom. Each of them also was sensitive to the social and political responsibilities of the school, especially since they believed that the school was educating for an unjust social order. The point has wide repercussions. Education affects the mind and therefore the quality of free choice in the political and social world. Total control over all the architecture of education might yield total domination.[57] The romantics believed that power had fallen into the hands of educators who served a social order that denied opportunity to the underprivileged. One does not have to agree with their social assessment to note the threat of an educational monopoly.

The insights of Kohl, Kozol, and Holt into classroom life may have been their most lasting contributions. All three critics have written further on education and have added to our understanding of the dynamics of classroom life. All warn, in words reminiscent of Waller, against self-satisfied teachers who believe that their superior knowledge will protect them against the unexpected. More critically, in their view, teachers rely on qualities not usually associated with a scientific assessment of knowledge. It would be simplistic to say that teaching is not a highly complex occupation that doesn't require a great deal of skill and knowledge to perform adequately. Yet the romantics seem to suggest that those skills must constantly be formed and reformed in the act of teaching, and that those skills cannot discount the importance of human compassion and concern for others. In their view, the image of the self-securing professional whose attainment of knowledge yields increased social status is particularly antithetical to the teacher's practice. The teacher's knowledge has value only insofar as it is given away. The teacher's authority and status has justification only insofar as the social and epistemological distance between the teacher and student is dissolved. The teacher's knowledge can never be hoarded; it must be shared and generously broadcast.

The romantic critique of the traditional school had several spinoffs. Kozol and Kohl later became involved in the free school movement. Holt became an advocate of home schooling. These schooling alternatives indicated a different type of student/teacher relationship that many believed was less authoritarian and built more around the intrinsic interests of the child. The free schools were designed to bridge the gap between the world and the child and to build sources of self-sufficiency and initiative in the student. In this way, dependence on "those who know better" might be lessened. Teachers were expected less to play the role of educational authority than to be "real people" who made mistakes and who might also learn from the student. As George Dennison, a central figure in the movement, explained, "We made much of freedom of choice and freedom of movement; and of reality of encounter between teachers and students; and of the continuum of persons by which we understand that parents, teachers, friends, neighbors, the life of the streets, form all one substance in the experience of the child."[58]

Ironically, many who were associated closely with the free school movement later criticized the stringency of an anti-authoritarian position. They argued that students living in a world that made little sense needed more structure and direction. If all adult intervention were withheld, students might lose a critical opportunity to gain a more secure sense of themselves within the social order. Kozol himself was later to criticize nondirective and nonimpositional forms of education, since they affirmed no commitment upon the part of the teachers and nourished no sense of social concern in the students.[59] In this critique, Kozol advanced the same argument for teacher intervention and involvement advocated by George S. Counts. In response to the refusal of teachers to take a more impositional role in the classroom, Kozol asked, "What loyalties can be constructed on the groundwork of desertion?"[60] The question cuts on more than one front, for one by one the romantics had abandoned the public school. What was to become of the millions of students who could not afford a private, "open" school or whose parents might not be able to educate them at home? What even had happened to the students whom the romantics had once taught in the public school? Years after Herbert Kohl had written his book about the thirty-six children he had taught in Harlem, many had dropped out. One of the children remarked, "Mr. Kohl one good year isn't enough."[61]

The most earnest and direct opponent of the public school was Ivan Illich. In reviewing his work, one finds a trenchant critique against the disabling power of knowledgeable elites, and it is in this context that his argument against the school should be understood. It cannot be forgotten that Illich was a former priest whose mission was grounded in serving the unfortunate and disenfranchised populations of Latin America. It is perhaps too easy to forget the tremendous investment in energy and resources public education represents, resources that developing countries and impoverished people can scarcely afford. Here, according to Illich, the increased expectations of the school harmed the poor in two ways. First, the message might be sent that education is a type of treatment administered in politically neutral settings by credentialed experts. This might cause attitudes of psychological impotence, further exacerbating feelings of dependence and inadequacy. Second, the message might be sent that education can occur only in certain settings, under certain conditions. Here education and schooling emerge as synonyms, with schooling requiring great sources of financial wealth. It soon becomes evident to the poor that extended schooling is out of their reach.

In this and other ways, Illich's analysis shocks us into the recognition that the form in which education is conducted carries a heavy message. In some senses, Illich believed that the school should be abandoned, not because it was working ineffectively, but because it was working well to prepare people for the subservience and deference necessary in a world run by experts. Illich no doubt overreacted to the power of experts, and some later sociologists have pointed out that experts may be victims of the bureaucratic order as much as lay people.[62] Nonetheless, a Deweyian message might be found even in the stridency of Illich's argument. Schools that are designed to prepare students for an active, intelligent, and participatory role in social affairs should not treat them as passive learners in the classroom. More than a little truth resides in the romantic belief that all learning is something that students have to do themselves; it is not something that should be done *to* them.

Illich's radical proposal received a good deal of criticism, some of it well deserved. Certainly the proposal to abolish schools took the argument for individual liberty to lengths to which even other romantics were not willing to go. Neil Postman, who had also written against the authoritarian teacher, believed that Illich himself was a type of authoritarian.[63] He meant that Illich tried to fit everyone within his particular conception of a just social order. It might be authoritarian and even mean-spirited to remove the opportunity for schooling from the millions of people who depend upon it daily. It might be authoritarian in another sense to turn over the direction of schools so completely to the interests of the young. Illich, like the other romantics, conceived of a utopian order in which students learned where, when, and how they liked. Yet as Arthur Pearl has noted, to learn what one likes is also to learn prejudices.[64] The romantics wrote as if the wisdom and experience of the teacher and the history and traditions out of which she operates should mean nothing to the child. In this sense the romantics were both anti-traditional and ahistorical. The romantics' affirmations of the inviolable nature of the child made it easier to give up on the school and to discount the past and present efforts of many to make the school a more humane and inclusive place to learn.

This raises a significant philosophical issue. The romantics, Illich in particular, suggest in their arguments a certain view of the autonomous individual that grew out of their Rousseauistic belief that children were born basically good. This faith leads them to be particularly sensitive to the perverting forces of outside social influences, but it also leads them to see the individual and society in perpetual conflict. The individual comes to be understood as an event of birth rather than as the creation of social and historical forces that might be embodied within the teacher.

While this view of the individual tends to promote a sense of heightened freedom, generally it is freedom conceived in its negative aspect. Freedom becomes defined as the area in which individuals are protected from the restrictions and manipulations of outside authority.[65] In this regard the thought of romantic critics closely parallels that of classical liberal thinkers whose understanding of the fallibility of human opinion led them to reject all uniform and authoritative answers to human problems. This view argues against experts having the one best answer to educational problems and against the imposition of expert authority.[66] On the other hand, the view provides no alternative, justified reason for the intervention of schools and teachers into the lives of students. All authority, whether expert or not, seems to fall before the demands of individual choice.

As we have seen in the thought of Illich, the unqualified celebration of the autonomous individual leaves little ground on which to base a school. This conclusion, despite Illich's profound radicalism, actually may reflect conservative tendencies. Illich's call for the end of public education closely follows the ideas of more conservative thinkers, who likewise believe that the school can no longer justify its monopoly over education. For example, in Milton Friedman's view, public schools should be abolished because only when market pressures are brought to bear on the inadequacies of schooling will education be improved.[67] Ironically, Myron Lieberman, long a staunch defender of a more exclusive and autonomous teaching profession, has also argued recently for discontinuing publically supported schools.[68] In Lieberman's view, the bureaucratic nature of public education not only interferes with student and parental choice, but also acts as a barrier to a more accountable teaching profession. Schools that have formed a more active relationship with private industry, which Lieberman refers to as entrepreneurial schools, will relieve the need to subject professional educators to overbearing state regulation. According to Lieberman, the professional standing of the teacher would be enhanced rather than negated by curtailing public education.

This indicates a final irony in the theory of the romantics. While some rejected schools out of a repugnance for a materialistic and self-serving capitalistic order, many others now advocate a similar abolishment of schools for opposite reasons. The abolishment of public schools might make education more susceptible to the entrepreneuerial spirit of profit, competition, and personal reward. Lieberman's idea is that competition among individual schools will lead to a greater emphasis on developing the technical skills necessary to teach more effectively.

Other thinkers have similarly attributed the development of modern professions as an expression of liberal individuality. The growth of modern professions occurred, according to Larson, as individuals were able to appropriate for themselves the knowledge necessary to practice in a free and open market.[69] Knowledge became a type of private property, like all properties more valuable as it became more scarce. Illich would like to make knowledge more accessible and shared, but in some ways the basis of his thought might produce some of the very excesses he is attempting to fight. The idea of an autonomous individuality, advanced by Illich and other romantics, contains within it no inherent barrier to the acquisitive self-interest that they deplore.

Five

The Modern Critique

The romantic critics brought into sharper focus issues critical to the consideration of the teacher as an expert. The question of expertise in education did not center only on the technical abilities of the teacher, though this was a significant issue; it centered also on the proper conceptual limits of a teacher's practice. The romantics' repugnance for the technical order merged with their belief in the sanctity of the individual to form a powerful criticism of authoritarian structures. Yet this sense of individualism resulted in a line of thought that discounted the authority of the teacher, whether that authority resulted from an assertion of expertise or from an assertion of the teacher's broader moral and cultural responsibilities. The romantic idea of an inviolable individualism seemed to imply that the teacher had to be morally neutral with regard to any interference in the life of the child. Freedom, conceived only in this negative aspect, could provide a strong argument against the authoritarian excesses of the expert teacher; but it could not provide a strong argument for forming the type of community upon which to build a school.

Ivan Illich took the romantic thought to its final conclusion in this regard. And while his argument relied too fully on the concept of an autonomous individuality, his analysis did make clear the significance of human agency in discussions of expertise. Critics like Manfred Stanley soon echoed Illich's concern by raising the question of dignity with respect to technological development.[1] In Stanley's formulation, dignity refers to the ability of people to have a creative or destructive effect on the world they inhabit, an ability that technological control over natural forces ultimately should have helped. Yet gigantic bureaucratic structures, the division of labor into protected specialties, and the incomprehensibility of expertise have all made dignity a great issue in technological writing.[2] In the same manner, Illich was sensitive to the position of the impoverished in society. He saw the school as part of a larger structure that did not provide the poor with access to the knowledge necessary to live whole and productive lives. Illich believed that the high economic and social status of professionals represented a new type of exclusive class privilege, clouded by the assertion of technical competence, but built around the advantages of wealth and power nonetheless.

This view of professions gained increasing prevalence in the 1970s and 1980s to the point that Donald A. Schon claimed that there existed a crisis of confidence in professional knowledge.[3] Schon noted that many more people have come to regard expertise with suspicion. Part of that suspicion is grounded in precisely the type of argument that Illich had raised. Some, for example, criticized the growing reliance on the credential as the mediator to expert service.[4] The point here was not simply the difficulty in finding a trustworthy expert, but determining whether the credential had unfairly limited the opportunities of the competent to practice. Randall Collins questioned the selflessness of professionals, since they tended to profit so much by their professed altruism.[5] But in some ways the profitable and exclusionary nature of professional jurisdiction seemed a natural outgrowth of technology itself.[6] Max Weber had noted long ago that technological development was inseparably bound to the growth in specialties.[7] This signified for the romantics the imperturbable and impervious nature of mammoth bureaucracies, but for scores of others it simply indicated the need to confine their vocational interest to a narrower area. One did not have to be a radical to see the economic benefit of exclusive expert knowledge.

Schon's contribution to this debate, however, went beyond debunking expert motives. He raised the question of whether the mode of technical rationality, upon which expertise had been built, could still so decisively inform professional practice. The romantics had also questioned technical rationality, but many times their critiques were couched in the hyperbolic celebration of the emotional and even irrational aspects of human judgment. While providing a deeper analysis of the excesses of professional privilege, Illich seemed to offer in response only the most simple espousal of individual liberation.[8] According to Schon, the more recent critique went much deeper and now reached into the ranks of the experts themselves. Professionals in many fields apparently now questioned whether expert knowledge could suffice to answer the types of ambiguous, changing, and uncertain situations in which they found themselves.[9] Technical rationality, Schon explained, was a direct result of the positivist belief that science could provide the answer to social and political problems.[10] This belief was also grounded in the idea that there was sufficient uniformity between problems in different contexts to justify the application of standard responses. As one writer on the professions explained it:

> If every professional problem were in all respects unique, solutions would be at best accidental, and therefore have nothing to do with expert knowledge. What we are suggesting, on the contrary, is that there are sufficient uniformities in problems and in devices for solving them to qualify the solvers as professionals...professionals apply very general principles, standardized knowledge, to concrete problems....[11]

Many professionals, far from celebrating an unmarred confidence in this mode of thinking, pointed to the lagging understandings, the unsuitable remedies, and the professional dilemmas that prevented the ready application of expert knowledge. The series of crises that plagued modern times—the increasing poverty, the deteriorating cities, the pollution of the environment—all seemed to resist the easy "technological fix." As Bruce Watkins and Roy Meader have pointed out, if it was clear that the romantic tendency to advocate the irrational response might lead to disaster, it was also clear that "most of the world's great problems will not have technological answers."[12]

Similarly, education theorists who did not necessarily share the romantic's ideology now began to argue that the vicissitudes of classroom life resisted the easy technical solution.[13] There seemed to be a new-found appreciation of the idiosyncratic nature of learning events, which always are mediated by the personalities and life histories of the participants and which always are unpredictable enough to confound the application of educational formulas.[14] More broadly, some now more deeply questioned the ability of schools to solve modern problems and to usher in the new age for which Counts and other progressives had long argued. The traditional disposition to see schools as panaceas for solving social problems had aided the movement to conceive of education as a field requiring greater expertise. As Henry Perkinson now pointed out, the historical effort to use the school to solve the problems of race, urbanization, and social mobility had not worked.[15] Driver education, sex education, and drug education programs testified to the enduring nature of the public's faith in school to ameliorate deep-seated social ills. Still, as the incidences of teenage pregnancy and of drug use continued to climb, it became less and less clear that the singular effort of expert educators could ultimately be effective.[16]

This skepticism indicated a new appreciation of the embeddedness of expert knowledge, of the fact that technical strategy was ultimately more deeply dependent on the situation in which it was used. Jacques Ellul had once characterized technical knowledge by its tendency to surpass cultural bonds. A "good" technique, he explained, was not tied to cultural traditions or to the character limitations of the person who employed it.[17] Interestingly, this type of thinking had underlain much of the research in teaching. Teacher educators believed that general principles of teacher effectiveness existed and could be applied in any situation, regardless of the disposition of the teacher and students.[18] But some critics in education and other fields were coming to doubt this proposition, especially since little firm evidence existed to tie teacher competence to extended formal training in teacher education programs.[19] On the other hand, on the job training, exactly the type of training that would place a teacher's knowledge and intelligence in a particular context, seemed to make a significant difference in teacher effectiveness.

As we have seen, these debates were not totally new. Historically, the belief that technical knowledge could provide the basis for a teacher's professionalism has been used to promote the place of teacher education as a separate and distinct discipline in university settings. This argument was still made, but some modern critics harkened back to James Bryant Conant's view that teacher education should be the domain of the entire university. No teaching of educational strategies could make up for a firm grounding in the academic disciplines, a grounding that not only seated the teacher within the larger frame of culture, but also helped exercise that general intelligence and capacity for judgment that was the mark of the good teacher.[20]

It should not be thought, however, that those who favored a more technical understanding of teaching were in full retreat. Despite the limitations pointed out above, it could reasonably be argued that the model of technical rationality had, if anything, gained in credibility since the romantics, for a brief moment, stole the educational spotlight. Behaviorism, programmed instruction, performance-based teacher education, and the effective school literature all lent credence to the idea that the teacher could be that professional accountable for educational success.[21] As we have seen, this understanding of a teacher's practice had a long and enduring history. It was this model of technical rationality that had led to the hierarchical structures recommended by early administrative progressives like Ellwood P. Cubberley. And it was this technical conception of educational practice that had in turn led educators to recommend that technical courses in pedagogy form the foundation of a teacher's training. It led reformers and critics like Daniel Lortie to repeatedly stress the standardized and secure knowledge base of teaching as a basis for the claims of teachers to professional status.

The most influential recent reports advocating reform in teacher education continued the tradition. The writers of the Holmes and Carnegie reports urged the abandonment of undergraduate teacher education and the adoption of more rigorous testing of prospective and practicing teachers, precisely, it seemed, because of their faith in the model of technical rationality. They argued that the technical skills demanded of the effective practitioner could now be based on secure scientific knowledge:

> ...the science of education promised by Dewey, Thorndike, and others at the turn of the century, has become more tangible. The behavioral sciences have been turned on the schools themselves, and not just in laboratory simulations. Studies of life in classrooms now make possible some convincing and counter-intuitive conclusions about schooling and pupil achievement.... Current literature demonstrates that well-meaning, and well-educated persons will make a number of predictable pedagogical mistakes that will disproportionately harm at risk pupils who traditionally do not do well in school, and who may be unlike their teachers in background and temperament.[22]

Thus, the modern backdrop for education writers critical of expertise included two horizons. On the right were those thinkers who continued to see education as a science and teachers as professionals who operate within the context of technical rationality. On the left was the romantic tradition, complete with its celebration of the nonquantifiable side of life—emotions, spontaneity, and intuition. The question of the individual and his relationship to society lit the entire scene. In some ways both vistas, the left and the right, saw society and the individual in perpetual conflict. If the romantic tended to free the individual from all teacher intervention, the advocates of expertise tended to make the individual subject to the increased care and authority of the expert. Like John Dewey, many current critics attempted to find some type of higher synthesis. The question they raised was whether teachers and education might benefit from the advances of technical know-how without violating the organic and contextual nature of human knowledge. What type of educational practice might honor the intellectual and moral capacity of both teachers and students? Below we continue our examination of the question of expertise and education with a brief review of the recent thought of Philip Jackson and Alan Tom, two theorists who, among others, have placed such concerns at the center of their work.

Philip Jackson

Even before Daniel Lortie had penned his influential study of teachers, Philip Jackson had written *Life in Classrooms*.[23] This work, unlike the work of Willard Waller and Lortie, attempted a more holistic interpretation of classroom life, describing it from both the position of the student and the teacher. The change of perspective was important both from a methodological and substantive point of view. Jackson held that the classroom was an incredibly complex place. One aspect of classroom life could not be considered apart from another. Consequently, he refrained from attempting to describe the classroom from one methodological perspective. In his opinion, no one method was sufficient. His book is an amalgam of anecdote, statistical study, interpretative interview, and "unquantifiable assertion."[24]

Jackson's approach allowed him to make insightful observations on how the conditions of the school affect student and teacher performance. The student, he argued, does not just learn directly from the teacher, but rather learns under a certain set of circumstances. The incredible amount of time the young spend in school (7,000 hours from kindergarten to seventh grade alone), as well as the uniformity and routine of the school environment, act to impress upon them a certain perception and to demand from them certain skills.[25] Students do not just learn to read and write; they learn to read and write in a crowd.[26] Students do not just learn how to behave appropriately; they learn how to behave under constant evaluation and under conditions that provide constant sources of distraction and diversion. Successful students do not just learn the prescribed curriculum; they learn the need to wait and the need to contain their desires until the appropriate moment.[27] Patience as much as knowledge is demanded of successful students. Successful students can tolerate mistakes and tolerate intermediate rewards. They learn to defer immediate desires, abandoning personal plans in order to take up with the designs of the teacher.[28]

The teacher's perspective is also shaped by the classroom environment. The classroom is an extremely busy and active place. Jackson noted that teachers engage in as many as 1,000 interpersonal exchanges each day.[29] This lends feelings of immediacy, urgency, and spontaneity to classroom life. The teachers whom Jackson interviewed relied on small, discrete observations to determine if students were learning or whether they were doing a good job. They tended to dismiss standardized tests as either an irrelevant nuisance or a flawed measure of student potential and accomplishment. Judgments in these matters were better made through personal day to day observations.[30]

Teachers stressed the informality of their classrooms, the importance of working and having an effect on individual students, and the need to have autonomy in their work.[31] Autonomy was seen not so much as the desire to be isolated and totally independent as the ability to determine classroom curriculum free from the unrequested invasion of outside administrators.[32]

Jackson noted that in the face of the great complexity of the classroom, the teachers he interviewed adopted an extremely simple approach.[33] Their talk was unmarked by a sophisticated vocabulary, just as their conceptions of why and how students learn were notable for their simplicity and lack of elaboration. Teachers tended toward the intuitive rather than the rational explanation, and they appeared to be so concerned with the immediate events of classroom life that they reflected very little on how classrooms or schools could be changed. While teachers were surprisingly confident and strong about their opinions on teaching, they rarely if ever turned to evidence beyond personal experience to justify their professional preferences.[34]

Jackson brought a considerable degree of balance to this description of teachers and students. The romantic critics used many of Jackson's insights to point out the repressive nature of the school environment and to emphasize the 'hidden curriculum' that would make students the passive recipients of expert care. Advocates of expertise, like Daniel Lortie, could point to the unthinking nature of teachers, to their lack of technical sophistication, and to their indifference to a technical subculture. The elements of conservatism and individualism that Lortie found so harmful to the development of teaching as a full profession appeared in Jackson's analysis in the simplicity of the teachers' reflections about pedagogical concerns.

Jackson was tempted by neither of these extremes of interpretation. He recognized the power of the teacher in the classroom and wondered if that type of authority was not after all consistent with what students would face in the real world. His appreciation of the context of teaching led him to ask whether the simplicity teachers showed toward their craft might not be a virtue rather than a vice.[35] On the face of it, Jackson admitted that the approach appeared strange. He too wished teachers would be more intelligent and considerate of the knowledge that underlay their craft. But the teachers whom he had interviewed were supposedly all experienced and highly recommended educators. If one accepted that fact, then the descriptions of teaching as a highly rationalized affair, as a mode of social engineering, might be wrongheaded.[36]

In these reflections, Jackson wandered far from the model of technical rationality upon which professional expertise is supposedly built. The knowledge appropriate to the craft, Jackson surmised, had to be more contextual and more responsive to the environment in which the teacher operated. Classrooms were not orderly places; they were characterized by human interactions that were unpredictable in both number and sequence. Jackson noted that a teacher facing such complexity and uncertainty must be intelligent, but it is an intelligence characterized by the ability to improvise, to react, and to think on one's feet. At the very least, the teacher must have a real tolerance for ambiguity.[37] In contrast to the quest for probability and predictability that marked the efforts of the hard-headed scientist, the worldview of the teachers seemed touched with an almost semimystical belief in the perfectability and ultimate potential of children. This idealism seemed quaint and tender-minded, and perhaps out of place in the austere, rationalized and controlled environment of the school. But Jackson believed that such idealism might be considered an antidote to the "toxic qualities of institutional life." He reasoned that a teacher, "by being less than completely rational and methodical in his dealings with students...may help to soften the impact of the impersonal institution."[38] The teacher presented students not with a model of an engineer, who had calculated in advance all the answers with great accuracy, but with a fallible human being. "In this way," he wrote, "the abstract goals of learning are given a human referent. Students cannot aspire to become a computer or a teaching machine or a textbook, but they can aspire to become a teacher."[39]

In his more recent writings, Jackson has wondered if the model of technical rationality, so prevalent in the research on teaching, has not begun to be reflected more in classroom life itself. Jackson notes that the practice of teaching is becoming more uniformly mimetic rather than transformative.[40] By this he means that the idea of education as a product is being stressed more than the idea of education as a process. In the present concern for observable and quantifiable results, for higher test scores, and for competency, the mimetic is ascendant. In this view of learning, memory skills and accurate feedback are essential. Jackson does not mean to discount this approach to a teacher's practice; it seems particularly valuable in math, sciences, and perhaps languages. Most research on teaching has, in fact, taken place in these types of classes. The insistence of pedagogical research to break down whole learning processes into manageable units is perhaps very helpful in these disciplines. However, for some types of learning, this approach seems inappropriate. If only the mimetic approach to teaching is emphasized, the whole range of education that deals mainly with the student's character is lost.[41]

The mimetic approach could also have unseen difficulties. The danger with a research method bent on discovering the secret behind good teaching is that it means "that the researchers will possess that knowledge before teachers themselves will."[42] This type of epistemic authority might not necessarily be abused, but the possibility exists that experts would once again attempt to control the learning situation from the top down. The danger is perhaps just as great in the classroom. Within the learning situation, the mimetic point of view makes the teacher an expert. The teacher is expected to have direct control over the subject matter and the methodological means to get the subject matter across. Jackson describes the students, by contrast, as doubly ignorant and doubly dependent:

> They neither know what the teacher knows, substantively speaking, nor do they know how to teach it in methodological terms. This dual condition of ignorance places them below the teacher epistemologically no matter where they stand regarding other social attributes and statuses.[43]

By contrast the relationships between teachers and students in the transformative tradition are not nearly so clear-cut. In this tradition, the object is a qualitative change in the person being taught, a metamorphosis in which the student is altered in some fundamental way. Values, traits, character, and attitudes are more the object of transformative teaching. Teachers are not expected to know the answer as much as to help discover the right questions. The methodology of the teacher who teaches in the transformative mode is completely different from the mimetic approach. Discussion, argumentation, and demonstration are used rather than didactic lecture. More crucially, the ends of the transformative teacher are different. Rather than skills and knowledge, the end of teaching is the change in the character of the student himself. This does not mean that the teacher does not profess to have knowledge; it is just that such knowledge is less an accomplishment than a search. The transformative teacher's authority is built less on what is known unequivocally than on what is known through constant revision and in constant quest of redefining knowledge through question and argument.[44]

As always, Jackson's overriding concern in describing the differences between the mimetic and transformative styles of teaching was not to recommend one uniformly over another but to suggest a balance. No teacher operated exclusively in the transformative mode. Indeed, one of the difficulties of the transformative mode was that it seemed idealistically to discount much of the prosaic and mundane duties that a teacher performed just to survive each day in the school. Nonetheless, Jackson argued, the transformative was present, if not in conscious strategy then at least in attitude, of those teachers who strived to inspire students to take more personal initiative, to question more, and to gain the ability to voice well-defined and substantive opinions. Jackson noted that it was the rare teacher who left one both intellectually stimulated and morally changed. Nonetheless, this clearly was the ideal of practice that he suggested.[45]

Alan Tom

Perhaps as much as any teacher educator, Alan Tom has made his mark as an incisive critic of the applied-science model of teacher research. More recently he has advocated another metaphor of teaching, teaching as a moral craft.[46] In his book of that title, he attempted to describe an understanding of a teacher's practice that might honor the intelligence necessary to teach without limiting pedagogy to a particular technical understanding. Teaching, he argued, is explicitly a moral enterprise and therefore requires capacities of commitment, care, and judgment as well as technical skill.

The trouble with the technical model of teaching, Tom argued, was that it was built on two false premises. The first premise was that there existed one best way of teaching. The research that attempted to describe universally applicable and universally effective teacher behaviors was founded on this premise.[47] The second premise was connected to the first; Tom described it as the "billiard-ball hypothesis."[48] This understanding of teaching asserted that a direct link existed between teacher behavior and student learning. The difficulty with this approach, Tom argued, was that it failed to take into account many of the mediating structures that determine learning.

Tom's analysis of the various attempts to discover an expertise of teaching demonstrated more particularly how the false premises operate. The existing research in teaching effectiveness, he explained, could be put on a continuum whose underlying variable is applicability. On the one end would be those attempts to identify teacher behaviors that might have generic application.[49] These attempts might include such law-like generalizations as Thorndike's principles of learning and those lists of teacher behaviors that research has shown to have the most beneficial effects on student accomplishment. On the other end would be research that attempts to take into account more than one variable in determining effective teacher strategies. Aptitude-treatment research is an example because it attempts to relate teacher tactics more precisely to the aptitude of students. The difficulty with the generic approach is that it has failed to produce conclusive evidence that one type of teacher behavior can succeed in all situations. The difficulty with the more context-specific approach is that it becomes impossible to determine and limit those variables that most effect learning.[50]

Tom used as an example the idea that student learning was increased when teachers used more direct instructional approaches in the classroom. This was deficient as a generic view of teaching because it failed to take into account differences in subject matter in which teacher dominance might be inappropriate. Also, some students learn better independently than being told what to do. Research that attempted to account for these different variables made some progress by postulating that instructional approaches should vary more with the situation. The direct approach seemed better for math, but not as good for art; it seemed better for reluctant learners, but not as good for self-starters. The difficulty, though, was that the complex of variables that might significantly affect the situation soon became so unwieldy as not to be helpful. For example, it is possible to find research recommending the direct approach for reluctant learners of normal emotional development in inner-city middle school social studies classes. In this example, the variables of grade level, emotional development, and situation are controlled, yet it still would not be clear that one had identified and allowed for all those variables that might impose themselves on the learning situation.[51]

Such difficulties, of course, have not prevented researchers from continuing their search. On the one hand, Tom was sympathetic to this, because the history of science was built upon the perseverance of thinkers who have profited from past failure. On the other hand, Tom wanted to raise theoretical and logical difficulties with the idea that teacher research might ever wholly solve the mystery of human learning. The first point he raised was cultural. He argued that teaching was a social event whose aims, purposes, and strategies were intimately connected to the way the educational enterprise was constructed.[52] The present method of universalized schooling indicated one way that modern people have solved the problem of education. But the strategy might change. To use the example of Illich, the community-based educational initiatives he proposed might altogether alter how effectiveness was judged. If frequent testing now seemed a particularly effective teacher behavior in the restricted environment of the school, it might be less prominent in the informal structures Illich recommended.

Second, Tom argued that teacher effectiveness research necessarily focused on the teacher rather than the student, making the latter a passive receptacle of teacher treatment.[53] As morally objectionable as that view might be (a point the romantics made often), Tom argued that such a perspective was also blatantly false. His argument related to the "billiard-ball" hypothesis mentioned above. The tendency to see a direct link between teacher action and student reaction failed to take into account how students affected teachers. Recent research points out that students develop sophisticated means to manipulate a teacher's responses.[54] Teachers found themselves constantly changing their responses to student behavior while students constantly changed their behavior to manipulate teacher responses. In addition, student perception of a teacher's behavior can make all the difference in a learning situation.[55] Many teachers using an aggressive approach of Socratic questioning have found that students with a fragile sense of self confidence view such efforts as subversive and destructive rather than as enlightening and invigorating.

Tom noted that it was precisely these difficulties that have now led some researchers to regard the best teachers as those whose "behavior is inherently unstable."[56] It has become more evident that:

> the effective teacher may be the one who is able to conceive of his teaching in purposeful terms, analyze a particular teaching problem, choose a teaching aproach that seems appropriate to the problem, attempt the approach, judge the results in relation to the original purpose, and reconsider either the teaching approach or the original purpose.[57]

This description seemed a long way from the search for certain and assured explanations of teacher–student interactions. Indeed, Tom argued that the very plasticity of the teaching situation and the changing dynamics of the classroom "suggest that the before-the-act teaching knowledge desired by teacher effectiveness researchers is not likely to be developed."[58]

In this second part of his argument Tom attempted to provide a model of teaching that differed substantially from the applied-science metaphor suggested by the teacher effectiveness researchers. He likened teaching to a moral craft and defined the term as "a reflective, diligent, and skillful approach toward the pursuit of desirable ends."[59] He argued that the normative dimension to a teacher's understanding of his practice was critical, not because educators might involve themselves intentionally with moral education, but because education itself was substantially a moral enterprise.[60] The unavoidable inequality between adults and children and the unavoidable control the teacher had over the process of learning led him to this conclusion. He also voiced some sympathy with the points of Hannah Arendt that essentially teachers are involved in the process of initiating the child into the world. This obligation was not to be neglected due to the facile belief that children were the equals of adults, and that they therefore did not require some substantial degree of assistance and direction.[61]

As controversial as such a discussion could be, Tom was plainly more nervous about the concept of teaching as a craft.[62] He realized that many theorists, Daniel Lortie among them, had pointed with dissatisfaction to the trial and error approach associated with the craft metaphor. The craft analogy supposedly stood in the way of conceiving of teaching as a full profession. It also supposedly implied that teaching was built around an apprenticeship system which, in its need to rely on uncodified traditions and on the direction of a mentor, was implicitly imitative and conservative. A craft in Tom's formulation was far more critical, more reflective, and more concerned with the body of knowledge and insights into practice that could inform reasonable pedagogy. The teacher, in his view, could not expect to rely on a type of knowledge that would solve problems beforehand but instead should pursue desirable learning goals skillfully and persistently.[63]

As Tom noted, metaphors are important tools in describing the practice of teaching. A metaphor provokes the practitioner to pay attention to some aspects of his work more than others and to develop and improve the capacity to practice in different ways.[64] Tom believed that the metaphor of a moral craft allowed teachers to profit from craft knowledge in a way that was at once reflective and vigorous without being confining. The normative dimension was critical, since the mere act of reflection described by other theorists might simply be conceived as an amoral technical activity. In Tom's own work as a teacher educator, the moral craft metaphor has been used to help students reflect on the context of their teaching, as well as on the types of problems they encounter in the classroom.[65] Pedagogical questions were just as important as answers in his view. The idea of moral craft allowed prospective teachers to ask particular questions not only about how to teach in certain situations, but also about how their teaching might contribute to the type of individuals they might wish their students to be.

Finally, the craft metaphor was important politically as a means for teacher educators to question the national direction of reform in teacher education. Tom has been a vocal critic of the National Council for the Accreditation of Teacher Education (NCATE), an organization that attempts to create and uphold standards that lead to national accreditation.[66] His appreciation of the context of teaching, and thus the context of teacher education, leads him to believe that the national standards employed by NCATE may be too procedural and technical. Again, the types of questions the standards provoke are just as important as the answers. In Tom's view, NCATE asks questions that could lead to mind-less conformity rather than serious reflection. They may encourage some to ask whether a program meets NCATE standards, not whether the program is based on a defensible conception of educational quality. Questions about whether the program helps teacher education students understand the normative dimensions of their practice may never be asked. Rather implicit in the NCATE standards is the view that form is more important than content, and even further, that one type of form is the best avenue for preparing teachers.[67] It is the neglect of moral peda-gogical reflection that Tom found repugnant in overly technical concep-tions of a teacher's practice. It is the view that there may be uniform ways of structuring teacher education that he finds objectionable in the NCATE standards.

Conclusion

It is a truism of history that some things never change. In the argu-ments pressed by Philip Jackson and Alan Tom one can see many of the concerns that had dominated the thought of previous educational thinkers. Both Jackson and Tom were sensitive to the type of top-down management of teachers that had been earlier advocated by the adminis-trative progressives and Ellwood Cubberley. Cubberley would, per-haps, be most impressed with the form that the schools had taken in the latter part of the twentieth century. The type of rationalized administra-tive structure and consolidated system for which he had worked was now largely in place. Of course, the question still remained of the teach-er's position within that structure, and it is with this issue that both Jackson and Tom were most concerned.

Both of these theorists found themselves adopting George Counts' counteracting belief that schools should not be run by those espousing just one ideological point of view. Jackson and Tom believed that sci-ence itself had become an ideology, an ideology that threatened to dom-inate the educational scene and so was all the more objectionable since it was not capable of attending to the terrific complexities of a teacher's practice. The ideology of science paid little attention to the teacher's moral and social obligations. In this sense, Jackson and Tom agreed with Counts that these concerns provided compelling reasons for cen-tering teacher training around courses that would make future teachers attend most directly to their larger public purpose.

Still, we can also identify some distinct differences in the views these last two theorists express. There exists in Tom and Jackson little of the faith, which was so apparent in both Counts and Cubberley, that the schools were the chief lever of social progress. Particularly in the writing of Counts, one gets the breathless impression that at any moment the world might fall or flourish due to decisions made in the school. Tom and Jackson lack as well the dramatic concern with social injustice so apparent in the romantic critique of public education. In the case of Tom, one discovers an urge to move beyond the critique of the school as a racist, sexist, and class-based institution to provide suggestions of reform that are more positive and helpful.[68] In the case of Jackson, one finds such an appreciation of the ambiguities of classroom life that the possibility of the teacher having a great and direct affect on larger social questions appears much less likely. In this way it might be argued that the greater sophistication of Tom and Jackson in understanding the limitations of educational expertise is purchased at a price. For even in the romantic critique of technical rationality and of the school as a repressive institution, there existed an awe of the great power those two forces were able to exert over the sensibilities and structure of human consciousness. For Tom and Jackson the teacher is neither an expert upon which to foist greater social obligations, nor a savior who might usher in the new age.

But then again there might be surprising benefits to this more reserved and balanced understanding of the teacher's authority. Tom, particularly, believes that a more accurate understanding of the teacher's practice as a moral craft will open up practitioners to the types of questions and reflection that will yield clearer, more morally responsible ways of working with students. Jackson, too, finds a redeeming grace in the flexibility, the simplicity, and the straightforward and tender-minded good will of teachers.

In this regard, it is possible to see the most distinct difference between Jackson and Daniel Lortie as they considered these same teacher characteristics. Where Lortie, in the glaring light of how other professions have reached for success, found only fault and lack of technical accomplishment, Jackson found reason to question whether the technical model was the most appropriate way to describe a teacher's practice. He asked whether the presumed faults of teachers might ultimately be virtues, and this in turn led him to consider the benefits of emotional sensibilities in an impersonal but interdependent environment. After all, there might be great power in the maligned sentiments of teachers—in humility, in attitudes of service, in the unrelenting faith in the potential of youth, and in the regard for process and commitment over product and quick satisfaction.

It must be noted that the language by which we describe the practice of teaching and the values on which it is built seems extremely important in this regard. This was a point that Tom in particular stressed, and in this context, Illich's distinction between Epimethian and Promethian man seems less fanciful after all. For if technical understanding of the teaching profession yielded certain expectations and raised particular issues, perhaps nontechnical and less exclusive understanding could yield another set of possibilities. The vocabulary of control, predictability, exclusiveness, probability, manufacture, product, power, effectiveness, autonomy, and competency comprise the lexicon of the teacher who would be expert. The emphasis on process, partnership, cooperation, service, flexibility, inclusiveness, participation, empowerment, and interdependence might provide the vocabulary of the educator for the new age.

This perspective would no doubt require new ways of understanding how teachers should go about their craft, of understanding about the structures in which they work and the ways in which they need to be educated. And it must be said that on this issue both Jackson and Tom are still somewhat incomplete. Hannah Arendt once said that it is easier for the modern person to say what he is against than what he is for, and in the writings of Tom and Jackson we can find this disposition.[69] Both thinkers, more than any other theorists we have examined in this study so far, subjected the positivistic model of expertise to critical scrutiny. They are against expertise conceived as the claim to a universally applicable technical skill. But what will take its place, and on what basis will the new authority of the teacher be founded? More particularly, what type of structures might be instituted to allow for the type of flexibility, choice, and sense of participation that expertise seems to discourage?

As a teacher educator Tom, more than Jackson, is directly concerned with these questions. He attempts to describe ways of going about preparing secondary education teachers that will give them the opportunity to reflect more deeply on the moral and social consequences of their work. This seems a great improvement over modes of instruction that would just focus on what works rather than on what the ends of instruction should be.[70] Tom has urged against adopting frameworks for teacher knowledge that fail to make explicit connections between technical questions and normative concerns.[71] Yet it is a possibility that Tom's proposals in that regard may be as morally neutral as the technical orientation to which he objects. Tom clearly realizes that teaching has a substantial and unavoidable moral component, but he gives too little indication about where a teacher's moral commitment should lie and on what ethical foundation it should rest. He commends the reflective teacher, but the reflective teacher presumably might reflect on morally dubious as well as morally ennobling facets of instruction.

Tom and Jackson clearly support more choice in teacher education. This stance is important, because if it is true that teacher educators do not yet know enough about how to construct effective programs, it seems important that at least there be room for experimentation. A single set of teacher education standards could be harmful in this regard. Both Tom and Jackson have vociferously objected to the recommendations of the Holmes and Carnegie reports partly for this reason.[72] Tom finds a political motive behind the idea that teacher education should follow one type of structure, and they both find arrogance and misinformation in the view that we at last know what particular strategies effectively and consistently lead to student learning. Both criticize the idea that the teacher should be understood only in terms of the other professions. Jackson pointedly remarks that the very idea that educators should be compared to doctors is degrading to teachers. Again we see Jackson finding virtue where others have found fault, discovering something particularly ennobling in the attitudes and sentiments of the dedicated teacher.

In this sense it is perhaps very important not to discount too quickly the professionalism of teachers merely because they have failed to live up to the modern model of an exclusive occupation built on a secure technical knowledge base. Historically, at least, this view of professions dates only to the nineteenth century, and some writers point out it is particularly prevalent in the United States and Great Britain.[73] Professions have a far older history, and one element not to be forgotten in this tradition is the attitude of service. This quality is scarcely mentioned in either the Holmes or Carnegie reports, presumably because it has been used to denigrate the intellectual qualities of teachers and to justify lower salaries. Nonetheless, in an age that some have described as narcissistic and that seems bent on securing personal advantage over public obligation, the element of service stands out as a very bright jewel indeed. Paul Goodman was one romantic who professed this more traditional view of the professional precisely because it seemed so out of step with the acquisitive society he found so distasteful.[74]

This suggests that teachers do themselves a great disservice by looking to others for the vision of what teaching should be. In this respect both Jackson and Tom emphasize the need for teachers to be more thoughtful about their practice and more imaginative in dealing with the particular problems that they face in teaching. Again, it seems that the idea of the teacher as expert, dependent on authoritative answers rather than questions, does not provide a good model for how the teacher must consider learning difficulties in the classroom. Donald Schon has recently advocated the idea of the reflective practitioner as a model for how many professionals might cope with the changing and haphazard nature of their practice.[75] And some educators have seized upon the idea as a way to describe good teaching. Surely this is very similar to the idea of intelligence and active consideration once advocated by Dewey and now advocated by Tom and Jackson. It is reasonable to speculate that even before Dewey, the best teachers engaged in practice that honored the mystery and possibility of learning, never denying the chance for their students to grow simply because it might conflict with a preconceived idea of how learning should proceed. Once again, one cannot help but recognize the inferiority complex of teachers as they must borrow from another source an idea that appears so crucial to an understanding of the classroom in the first place.

Looking more closely at themselves and other practitioners would require that teachers pay more attention to the history of their craft and to the individual teachers who have done it well. Both Tom and Jackson recommend both an increased appreciation of the foundations of education and an increased emphasis on the writings and reflections of fellow teachers. Tom, in particular, sees great merit in the insights offered by Herbert Kohl on how to overcome some of the problems of instruction.[76] In this area it might be said that the romantics made one of their more lasting contributions to teaching. Kohl, Kozol, and Holt all provided detailed descriptions, not just of the evils of the school, but also of the problems they encountered as they tried to teach successfully. Until his death, Holt encouraged teachers to publish in his magazine those insights that might help their colleagues. As Tom and Jackson would argue, such suggestions could not be considered answers, but they could be considered guides to practice. In that way they might be one avenue to increasing the knowledge and the collegiality which remain so important to the formation and practice of a profession.

Six

Expertise, Postmodernism, and Critical Pedagogy: The Search for the Public Good

In the most fundamental sense, the rule of the expert represents an appeal to authority, the authority of privileged knowledge. From the progressives to the modern professionals the question of authority has been primarily understood in scientific terms.[1] The escape from tradition, the growth of democracy, and the great advances in science and technology all seemed to make such an understanding reasonable and positive. Yet as we have seen, the supremacy of science as a way of understanding the world has not gone unchallenged. The romantic worldview, with its roots deep within the democratic and pastoral traditions of American life, provides a critique of science based on the celebration of spiritual and emotional self-creation. The view of education provided by Alan Tom and Philip Jackson has a romantic side. Much more than most romantics, however, they are concerned with the messy pragmatics and contingencies of educational practice. Here their thinking resembles in part a growing suspicion of the professions and of expertise generally, as practitioners in many fields attempt to come to grips with the vacillating and original nature of professional practice.[2]

In the late 1980s, the modern critique of science has expanded to include an even more complex discussion over the authority of knowledge. This critique includes and has in part grown out of a larger movement loosely termed "postmodernism."[3] Ironically, much of what is called the "postmodern critique" issues from the advances of science, particularly in the areas connected with information and communication technology. It has been common in light of these advances to speak of the information age or computer age in which change has become so rapid and the increase in human knowledge so overwhelming and powerful that the secure base of knowledge itself is called into question. Knowledge, according to Jean-François Lyotard, is not simply a matter of quality, knowledge perceived as good for its own sake.[4] Rather, knowledge is a matter of quantity, a commodity to be bought or sold, traded or monopolized consistent with the conditions imposed by the languages of the computer and by the influences and constraints of the marketplace. Lyotard theorizes that nations increasingly will fight over knowledge in the same way they once fought over land. In this way, knowledge will become more and more a question of power and government as conscious decisions are made about who decides what knowledge is and what inquiries need to be pursued.

Of course, the correlation of knowledge with power is by no means new. It has been a central pillar in the social project of expertise, the need to formulate that specific understanding of knowledge that underlies professional practice and reserves it for a particular group.[5] What is newly emphasized in the "postmodern age" that Lyotard describes is a growing skepticism that knowledge has a solid foundation, either philosophical or scientific, that can duly account for the plurality of voice and opinion found in a more linguistically diverse society.[6] With this skepticism comes the belief that knowledge has been and continues to be in the service of elite groups who can control information resources or define what counts as legitimate cultural expression. This power can operate overtly, as when the culture of minorities, women, or 'the lower classes' is discounted and the divide between high and low culture is made more manifest; and it can operate insidiously, as when the mass media so trivializes information and news as to render all knowledge and significant public debate a matter of entertainment or style.[7]

In expressing these doubts and in exposing what is seen as the oppressive manipulation of discourse and intelligence, much of postmodern writing is penned as a type of protest and opposition. Yet on the positive side, there is a celebration of plurality, bringing recognition and respect to the many areas of understanding that should comprise the human conversation. This aspect of postmodernism pivots on the understanding that all types of knowledge are really types of languages in competition and even in opposition to one another.[8] Thus, the language of science with its insistence on concensus, measurable results, and objectivity operates in sharp distinction to those narratives that emphasize particularity, diversity, and subjectivity.[9] The language of the Enlightenment—with its focus on progress, the unfolding of history, and on reason—is challenged by discourses that discount the guiding structures of traditionally fixed referents and that understand values to be conditional, relative, and problematic. The modernist belief in the control and subjugation of nature, viewed as masculine and hierarchical, is opposed by discourses that celebrate interdependent and caring relations, viewed as feminine and reciprocal.

The challenge of postmodernist views to the rule of the expert is both straightforward and complex. Expertise is challenged on both the scientific and institutional level by the view that all knowledge is conditional and problematic. Lyotard, for example, takes pains to describe himself as philosopher and not an expert, since an expert is in the business of knowing and concluding while a philosopher is in the business of doubting and questioning.[10] Similarly, Richard Rorty would undermine the place of authority in philosophy by arguing that as a discipline it must give up the project of establishing a fixed, universal, and transcendent reference point upon which to ground knowledge and capacities for human judgment.[11] In the pluralistic world that Rorty describes, philosophy has more in common with literature than science. The hero is not the expert but the artist or poet who understands the language of contingency and is able to make her mark upon the world without appeal to literal fact or universal truth.[12]

These views have obvious and significant implications for education, the impact of which is only beginning to be felt. Most notable (though perhaps not most accurately characterized as postmodern), is the feminist writing that seeks to expose masculine biases in the institutional structure of schooling and in curriculum and instructional theory. Carol Gilligan, Madeline Grumet, Jo Anne Pagano, Nel Noddings, and others have made clear that the emphasis on hierarchical relations and abstract knowledge, so central to expert relations, stands in opposition to points of view based on immediacy, care, and mutuality.[13] Gilligan's classic critique of the theories of moral development espoused by Lawrence Kohlberg is also a profound critique of expertise. Kohlberg believed that moral development is connected to cognitive development.[14] It can be described in terms of discrete and universally applicable stages, each succeeding stage representing a higher progression toward more abstract moral reasoning. In opposition to this 'masculine' view, Gilligan postulates the 'feminine' understanding of relations fostered by feelings of cooperation, affection, and concern. Rather than positing an ascendant type of moral knowledge based on detached principle, Gilligan asserts that women typically reason another way. They focus on the immediacy of the situation and on the protection of the individual as well as the solidarity of the group. While the sociology of expert is bound up in specialism and autonomy and thus in the social need to cultivate the kindnesses of strangers, the psychology that Gilligan describes is bound up in cultivating the affection and responsibility that comes from dialogue, concern, and intimacy.[15]

Another important contribution of postmodernism to educational theory has occurred in the continuing debate over school reform. Postmodernism generally advocates a type of antifoundationalism, a philosophical critique of all knowledge systems that preclude change and variety on the basis of predetermined understanding and conclusions. Postmodernist views loom as direct challenges to conservative reform projects that try to establish teacher education according to a more specifically defined knowledge base. They also loom as direct challenges to those who believe that teachers must adopt the role of cultural experts. Here some argue that teachers need to be more in command of understanding and transmitting the artistic and literary traditions deemed to be most legitimate and worthy.[16] For this reason, postmodernism of every stripe has earned the wrath of conservatives, who have argued the most vehemently for some return to tradition and to the study of the "great books" of Western literature. In the view of the most evangelistic of conservative critics, Allan Bloom, postmodernism represents "the last, predictable stage in the suppression of reason and the denial of the possibility of truth."[17] In the view of Daniel Bell, postmodernism only accentuates the modern tendencies toward hedonism and self-destruction.[18]

The shrillness of such language need not blind us to the complexity of the philosophical issues that now help frame current debates in educational theory. For example, it can be argued that the conservative position actually represents the opposing side of the postmodern debate over knowledge. Both views rest on the implicit belief that the Western heritage is in a general state of social and moral disruption and that the traditional sources of cultural authority have been overturned. In sharp contrast to the postmodernist position, the conservative project has been to reestablish and replenish the vitality of tradition rather than to ease and celebrate its passing.[19] Many came to see the failing of the schools in the context of a larger social and economic crisis. In the years dominated by the Reagan and Bush administrations, the national conservative political agenda has been to restore confidence in the power of the United States in political affairs and in the world market. The schools have been seen as the lever to make such restoration possible.

The conservative position has generally supported the idea of expertise, because it argues for increased technical skills and understands the moral, social, and political concerns of education as depending more on a uniform cultural competence than on matters of social awareness and critical reflection. This view stands in sharp contrast to the tradition of

education that would emphasize thinking skills and would base instruction and curriculum on participation and student experience. Yet the
conservative position became dominant in the 1980s and early 1990s in
part because its social analysis seemed to be supported from the left.
Such thinkers as Robert Bellah and Christopher Lasch agreed with conservative thinkers that the loss of a commonly held sense of value had
negative effects on sources of public responsibility.[20] Whereas conservative critiques lamented the corresponding lack of respect for convention
and tradition, liberals lamented the sapping of political will as people
failed to understand and articulate public obligations. Lasch, who has
been a strong critic of expertise in the self-interested form it has taken in
modern professions, held that the value of extreme individualism has
resulted in a culture in which people fall back on strategies of survival.[21]
This serves to give increased power to the expert. Rather than feeling
compelled or able to unite in concerted political action, people relinquish
political power to technical specialists.

For many educational theorists, especially those who do not wishs to
abandon the public conversation to the conservatives, an acknowledg-
ment of the fragmented moral character of public life presents a substantial theoretical dilemma.[22] On the one hand, the dilemma is political and
relates to the possibility of political and social commitment in a world that
continues to be characterized by inequality and oppression. On the other
hand, the argument is moral and presents the problem of establishing and
transmitting some vision of public life upon which to base an understanding of teaching and a democratic pedagogy. The problem in this case
entails establishing a sense of teaching authority that avoids the doctrinaire traps of tradition without falling prey to that sense of professionalism and expertise that in Thomas Haskell's words might "exchange general citizenship in society for membership in the community of the
competent."[23] For our purposes, the central question of expertise, given
the reality of an indeterminate world, seems simple and yet incredibly
difficult: how might our understanding of the teacher depend upon and
yet help construct a communal sense of the public good? Maxine Greene
and Henry Giroux have constructed two contemporary visions around
the dual but connected languages of personal liberation and political
action. The teacher conceived as stranger and the teacher conceived as
transformative intellectual now become the focus of our concern.

Maxine Greene and the Teacher as Stranger

It is not altogether easy to understand strangeness as a characteristic
that might inform a conception of teaching. Instruction in many ways

depends on overcoming strangeness, both in the way the teacher and the student relate interpersonally and in the way the mystery of subject matter is dissolved by the event of learning. As a social category, the stranger is the outsider or the person who has yet to be initiated into the conversation of the community. Students are strangers in the sense that they are uninformed or still need to be shaped to make them recognizable as full human beings. In response, teachers who are strangers loom as a threat and an anomaly. They seem particularly ill-equipped to carry out their responsibilities, being unfamiliar to those who must give them their trust and being uninformed of the understanding they are pledged to transmit.

As an understanding of the modern world, however, the category of strangeness appears more and more applicable. One need not evoke the incredible social change, the technological mystification, and the confusion over values to appreciate modern obscurity. One need only contemplate the fluidity of modern lives increasingly marked by changes in personal allegiances, by flexible careers, and by constant mobility. In this way, nearly everyone has experienced what it means to be a stranger and has experienced the incapacities, ambiguities, and doubts that go with the condition. As an aspect of bureaucratic life, strangeness is found in the labyrinth of official territory and in the complexity of particular policy and responsibility. Within the massive and inpenetrable structures that comprise modern institutions, strangeness can become a source of futility, powerlessness, and despair. Of course, modern enigmas, like the mysteries of old, have their own antidotes and correctives, their own priesthoods possessed of the ability to peer into the unfathomable and interpret its contents. From the lay perspective, strangeness is the natural element of the expert. In possession of the secret and capable of seeing through the intricate mass of conflicting information, belief, and symptom, the modern expert can help treat confusion and perplexity. Here strangeness is not so much dissolved or overcome as ameliorated and reaffirmed. In many ways the expert is the perfect complement to a world built upon indeterminacy, a type of minister who tends to modern confusion but is only at home and vital within the web of its entanglement.

When Maxine Greene wrote *The Teacher as Stranger* in 1973, she wished less to comment on the possibility of overcoming strangeness than to accentuate and describe the extent of its interminability.[24] Influenced most by John Dewey and various existentialist writers, she came to this task particularly informed. Dewey had noted the futility of any quest for certainty and had based an understanding of learning less on finding ultimate answers than on reacting intelligently and reflectively to immediate problems. Existentialism, in general, had emphasized "existence over essence," stressing the freedom of the human being to determine and shape reality and to be, in Sartre's words, "responsible for everything." For Greene, who once described herself as a phenomenological existentialist, reality is never assured, certain, or determined. Rather, reality is always mediated and always structured by the design of individuals, who by choosing freely can act positively within the world to shape its future.

From this point of view the strangeness of the world takes on a natural disposition. It certainly results from the oblique pressures of massive institutions since they foster a kind of heedlessness of personal responsibility or tend to reduce judgment and action to matters of policy and mechanical function. More importantly, however, it results from the character of the world's even more fundamental indeterminacy. The writing of Maxine Greene has a characteristic style that seems at one with this most salient point. Her prose is marked by constant quotations from the wisdom literature of philosophy, literature, and social science. In the midst of this vast expanse of literary and philosophical allusion it becomes increasingly clear that the perceived world is always open to change and to various ways of sense making, and that the character and form of the world are, therefore, open to the possibility of reflection and intelligent response. It is in this way that Greene seeks to point out that a fundamentally shapeless world need not be unintelligible or incomprehensible. Indeed, it is possible to capture much of the essence of Greene's philosophy by noting two prominent considerations: first, her affection for examining the various ways different thinkers have interpreted the world; and second, her imperative that teachers confront their own life stories in pursuing exactly the same project of individual reflection and action.

Such concerns have always played a significant role in her thought. When she wrote the *The Public School and the Private Vision* in 1965, she had already displayed her ongoing interest in the arts and particularly in the life perspectives of artists.[25] A literary artist, she noted, is "characteristically concerned with presenting his personal experience of life, his individual confrontations with tension and change."[26] In this way, artists provide not only an inexhaustible source of comment upon a reality that for most people has become unproblematic and routine, but also moral models by which teachers might measure their own responsibilities. Artists find they must rebel against received authority as part of the effort to uncover their own voice and vision. Like artists, teachers also must examine unchallenged preoccupations and expectations:

> The teacher can no longer simply accept what is transmitted by 'experts' and feel he is properly equipped to interpret the world. He cannot even rely on the authority of accumulated knowledge or the conventional wisdom on which so many people depend. He must make decisions of principle, which make necessary a definition of new principles, more relevant norms and rules. Therefore, he must become accustomed to unconventional presentation of situations around him, to ways of talking with which textbooks cannot deal. Only if he breaks with fixed, customary modes of seeing can he remove the blinders of complacency. Only then can he take responsibility for his pursuits of norms and meanings.[27]

Taking moral responsibility means, in Greene's view, that teachers have to undertake a substantially philosophical project. In a real sense, they have to become active philosophers, adept at questioning meaning and reflecting on experience. This understanding of philosophy differs considerably from the view that philosophy as a discipline composes a received body of wisdom, or the view that philosophers are systematic thinkers to whom teachers can appeal for truth and knowledge about what is ultimately best in teaching situations.[28] Rather to think philosophically means to be involved in basically the same project of reflection and creative action that Greene had ascribed to artists. Here Greene develops a conception of philosophy and a type of philosophical project remarkably similar to that offered by Richard Rorty. In this view, philosophy is allied much closer to the arts than to the sciences. The rigor of philosophy lies less in developing holistic systems or edifices of closely reasoned argument than in seeking companionship and guidance in story, narrative, and the world of ideas. Rather than trying to finally determine the 'truth' in a conclusive sense, the teacher instead would become involved in constantly trying to "build a multi-faceted stock of knowledge, a multiplicity of constructs he can use to order his experience."[29]

Of course, in its own way this makes great intellectual and creative demands on the teacher. While the teacher can be neither expert nor the recipient of a guiding expertise, she must still read widely, think deeply, and react imaginatively. The effort at being awake to the world and existentially present in it has its own rewards. As teachers come to see reality from the different points of view provided them by artists and philosophers, they will find themselves "living in a progressively more meaningful world."[30] But again, this depends on developing a genuinely thoughtful attitude. Teachers can not simply mimic the views of others or internalize them in the sense recommended by those writing from a Freudian tradition. Neither can they subsume the actual conflict implied by the life and thought of artists in an effort to meet the demands for cultural literacy. Rather, they have to be personally involved in the artistic and philosophic process, bringing imagination and intelligence to bear on the contraints and obstacles of their own lived situations. They have to engage in an authentic search, a search that leaves them open to encounter "that jolt which comes when one's sense of the world is challenged."[31]

This whole process is admittedly introspective. It involves what Greene, following Hannah Arendt, has called "a soundless dialogue," "through which (as it were) we talk things over with ourselves."[32] Consequently it is proper to wonder if this project of continual reflection represents simply another aspect of the modern obsession with self-involvement and narcissism or whether it represents a real alternative. Greene answers this by connecting her understanding of freedom with an understanding of care. Freedom in this sense is not an escape from responsibility or from the obstacles and conditions that confront each of us daily.[33] Rather, freedom entails our ability to be alive to the possibilities of the world and to bring such possibilities to actuality. By being actively engaged, teachers and students work to escape the alienation from the public world that results when people rely on unexamined convention, technical solution, or bureaucratic policy. Instead of feeling helpless in the face of received authority, the reflective student and teacher are more likely to feel empowered and free. Freedom, Greene argues, must be conceived dialectically, always in relation to those oppositional forces that might constrain choice and prevent people from challenging that which is conceived as natural or unproblematic. The idea of autonomous individual is a myth, since people "always have to confront a certain weight in lived situations, if only the weight of memory and the past."[34] It is only through such confrontations that people can simultaneously engage in acts of self creation and social commitment, freedom being in this way both personal and social. As Greene notes, "Freedom shows itself or comes into being when individuals come together in a particular way, when they are authentically present to one another (without masks, pretenses, badges of office), when they have a project they can mutually pursue."[35]

The pedagogical implications of such commitments are both obvious and significant. As the teacher through reflection and choice begins "to create himself as a human being," he becomes "capable of freeing other human beings to choose themselves."[36] The teacher can bring a 'personal' knowledge to bear on instructional circumstance. Such knowledge is not so much private as it is owned and genuinely related to the teacher's own life situation.[37] A genuinely reflective teacher presents students with a model of an authentic learner truly present in the learning event. Her presence is not mediated by unexamined convention or by the need to impose views of the world that have little to do with the emancipatory struggle of students. Indeed, if the teacher in the advocacy of her own commitment and understanding simply encourages students to adopt her view, then it can be said that as an educator she has failed. Greene applied this principle to her own philosophical project and her own work as a teacher, since even her advocacy of freedom and philosophical reflection needed to be held up for criticism. Referring to *The Teacher as Stranger,* she wrote, "This book will have been a failure if having read it, those with different backgrounds and orientations simply adopt or appropriate the selective vision they find presented here."[38]

Of course, this presents both Greene and the teachers who might follow her with difficult problems, especially with regard to matters of value and the search for the public good. Specifically, the matter comes to bear on teachers who must act on their own passionately held beliefs and yet provide space for students to come to terms with their own sense of the world and their own sense of commitment. Generally, the matter comes to bear as people begin to recognize the need to be less self-regarding and to form enduring relationships based on intersubjectivity and interdependence. In either case, Greene sees it as wrong to impose one's own value, and yet she also sees it as wrong to allow conventionally held views which might reflect racist, sexist, or other inhumane biases to go either personally or institutionally unchallenged.[39] Characteristically, her response to the dilemma is not to evoke an answer or an argument, but to acknowledge the problematic in all its unavoidable human complexity:

> Complicated problems confront any teacher who attempts "moral education." If he believes, as positivist philosophers do, that only principles can be taught, along with the nature of good reasons, he still must determine which principles can be made meaningful to the contemporary young. He must determine what sorts of actions have "moral resonance," which do not and which should not. If he considers that guidelines are impossible to define any longer, if he is more concerned with the way people respond to appeals from "conscience" and the way they create themselves as norm-regarding beings, he will still find himself in tension as

he watches individuals do violent and careless things. And, indeed, no matter what his philosophical approach, the teacher cannot help recognize that human beings are always capable of hatred and bigotries, that it is difficult for anyone not to falsify himself. Whether he tries consistently to remain "calm and cool" in the knowledge "that the way of life he prefers, all things considered, includes the moral way of life," whether he chooses to live "in unsatisfied indignation" because "too high a price is asked for harmony," he will find himself entangled in the problematic haunted by open questions. In his capacity as teacher he is expected to know the answers, to have prescriptions at hand which tell the young how they ought to live. Unable to tolerate major personal uncertainties when he is engaged in teaching, he is likely to tell himself that he does indeed have it all worked out, that he knows.[40]

Such an answer is not likely to please philosophers who require more clarity or rigorously argued responses. Yet the answer does reflect a certain consistency and does call for a type of moral courage. The consistency is founded again on the perception that the world is and always will be a human construction, dependent upon the will and ability of human beings to shape its contours. The courage is founded on the disposition to face clearly the freedom and responsibility that such a view of the world requires. Greene constantly warns against the various temptations and failings, both individual and institutional, that might subvert the integrity of the teaching act. "The teacher," she writes, "is continually being asked to write a pious and authoritative role for himself and submissive or savage roles for the young people he teaches."[41] Pretending to know, the teacher falls back on perceptions of craft that are excessively technical or managerial, in which teachers are conceived as learned authorities and students are perceived as "deficit systems, empty vessels awaiting our ministrations."[42] She notes that we are not likely to "empower students...if we cannot posit them as free agents, persons with the capacity to choose to learn."

Under this view teachers must come to face realistically the limits of their expertise and authority as they relate to a proper understanding of the teaching craft. Agreeing with Michael Polanyi, she remarks that much of what we know about teaching seems intuitive, lying below the surface as a type of tacit knowledge that nonetheless seems decisive.[43] This does not mean that the conceptions of learning generated by the social sciences cannot and should not inform our teaching. Rather, it means imaginatively incorporating the findings of the social sciences into our understanding. Hence they are less prescriptions and rules than tools to help teachers govern a course of action.[44] Even more importantly, they should not blind teachers to the normative dimensions of their craft and particularly not to their obligations to attend to the needs of students to find their own meanings and pursue their own possibilities.

Again, this philosophy imposes upon the teacher its own type of discipline and rigor. Teachers, following Greene's prescriptions, are warned against attempting to order affairs more or less mechanically and manipulatively and against appealing only to privileged knowledge for status and authority. Green notes that "any person who teaches understands what it means to feel oneself to be an 'authority' with respect to what one is trying to teach."[45] But she quickly remarks that most of us realize "that our authority or authoritativeness is likely to be acknowledged by our students only when they need help in becoming, in pursuing what they desire to pursue." It is a mistake in this regard to believe that students are wholly dependent or that learning results in a direct way from teaching. Rather, students have their own "legitimate (and sometimes illuminating) ways of constructing realities." All too often these realities have escaped notice or have been blatantly disregarded as in the case of black children and the case of girls and women. Learning goes beyond what is taught:

> ...some of us have the courage to recognize that individual (like cooperative) learning transcends teacher planning and control. If we are "successful" or "effective," then, there will be no visible product for which we can take credit. There will be diverse individuals in diverse contexts, engaging in continually new beginnings as they work to make sense of their worlds.[46]

In the final analysis, it is the celebration of life's varied possibilities that is conclusive for Greene's account of pedagogy. In one sense, she wishes for students what she wishes for herself, the opportunity "to read at least one tenth of what I'd like to read" and like a stranger to "look inquiringly and wonderingly at the new world one encounters." In this view, even Greene's own obvious love and regard for the classic literary and philosophic texts take on a tentative character in her description of the teaching event. She realizes, along with Allan Bloom and E. D. Hirsch, the possibility that the world threatens to become a society of strangers and laments the lack of a public sphere in modern life. Yet in distinction from Bloom and Hirsch, she holds that to press uncritically a monolithic (and patriarchal) view of literacy is to deny the very basis upon which great works of art become paradigm cases, exemplary in the sense that they provide openings to alternative realities. Writing of the great works of art, she notes:

> It is not that we are morally "better" or possess more status when we know these things. It is that, through our own attending...we are able to break the bonds of the ordinary.... And that is what some of us, considering our craft want for those we teach: the opportunity and the capacity to reach beyond, to move toward what is not yet.[47]

In the philosophy of Maxine Greene, the teacher, like the expert, acknowledges and even flourishes amid a world that has become increasingly strange. Like the expert, the teacher must find legitimate status and responsibility in consideration of the issues of knowledge, power, and authority. Yet where the expert confronts a perplexing world as a type of riddle or problem open to expert solution, the teacher refuses to dissolve mystery in the name of competence. The category of the strange in this latter context represents a place of opportunity and wonder rather than a forum for resolution. The distinction, as Greene warns us, is not easy to draw. In the face of befuddlement, it is tempting to define a sense of self in terms of what one finally knows. From Greene's perspective, this can be deadly not only to the life of the mind, but to the senses of caring, relation, and thoughtfulness that are so vital to classroom life. An expert, she seems to say, defines herself primarily by what she knows; a teacher primarily by what she doesn't.

Critical Pedagogy and Expertise

It is possible to understand the philosophy of Maxine Greene as one built on discontent and disruption. Like many of the progressive thinkers, she too sees possibilities for learning opening up in precisely those places where the securities of convention and tradition have been challenged or dissolved. Greene is constantly sensitive to the conditions that promote a type of mental stupor and powerlessness in students and teachers. For this reason, her thought provides a critique of the expert metaphor insofar as it emphasizes an authoritarian connection between knowledge and power and hinders the freshness and creative potential of the learning relationship. In this sense, she is sensitive to the institutional forms of repression that have denied the voices of the weak and impoverished and established barriers to the search for self-creation.

Despite these valid and humane concerns, the center of Greene's thought is less political than philosophic. The directions it pursues are closer to a personal search than a public mission.[48] It is impossible not to note how much of the disruptive world for Greene is bound up in literature, in comment and reflection on the world rather than the world itself. Thus, even in the appeal to literature, the emphasis is on ideas and their transformative and creative import rather than on the condition of the world and its deterministic and conforming power.

Discontent can be understood in different ways. Paulo Friere, for example, has conceived of education in frankly political terms.[49] In his ground-breaking and remarkable work of educating impoverished people in Brazil and elsewhere, Friere found that the lives of the poor were circumscribed not only by their illiteracy, but also by their failure to see themselves as autonomous and empowered political beings. Friere's pedagogy revolved around the dialogical relationship he was able to form with his students that avoided domination and manipulation. Rather than seeing the peasants as objects to receive his expert instruction and guidance, he encouraged students to reflect on their own political and social situations. In this way, they discovered the words that had meaning for their own lives and for their struggle for liberation. These words became the foundation for a literacy of both technical proficiency and political awareness. Thus, Friere's pedagogy intended to disrupt not only the student's own silent world, but eventually also the objective conditions of society.

For over ten years a small group of educators have built upon Friere's ideas as well as the ideas of other social theorists to fashion what is variously termed "critical education", "critical theory," or "critical pedagogy."[50] Critical theory is founded first and foremost on a certain analysis of the history and sociology of schooling.[51] When E. P. Cubberley fashioned his history of schooling, he worked from assumptions that allied history with evolution and with the progressive idea that public education and the development of institutionalized, state-supported schooling was the culmination of years of struggle against the forces of ignorance and evil. Schooling, in this view, was allied with democracy and equal opportunity. But for many revisionist historians writing in the 1960s and 1970s, schooling had a far darker history. Schooling in their view is intimately tied to property interests and the need for social control. For the revisionist historians and for later critical theorists, schooling is an institution that primarily serves conservative interests, ensuring the continued dominance and wealth of the powerful.

This reading of history has its roots in a sociological understanding of class struggle. From the conservative point of view, schools can be seen as the agency of equal opportunity, one that allows for social mobility and the expression of individual potential. Yet from the point of view of critical theorists, the instructional practices of the school serve in large part to reaffirm social class and to erect barriers to cultural expression.[52] Such thought has profound implications for the understanding of expertise, especially as competence becomes tied to credential and opportunity becomes more carefully controlled and extended. Expertise, in this view, can easily become part of a web of social and political relations that reproduces the existing economic structure and that prepares working-class people for subordinate positions in the marketplace. Culturally, expertise can become part of an epistemological foundation that would legitimize and canonize dominant forms of expression to the detriment of other voices and minority points of view.[53] Experts, therefore, become not only recipients of a credentialing system that would reserve for them the highest social and economic positions, but also judges of what constitutes worthy art, literature, and music. In short, they become caretakers of the 'appropriate' ways to understand the world.

What distinguishes many critical theorists is their desire to use this ideological position to understand and transform the practical aspects of schooling. According to the critical tradition, authoritarian instructional practices that overtly prepare students simply to be good and obedient workers neglect democratic virtues connected with reflectivity and honoring public obligations. An understanding of the oppressive nature of schooling obligates both teachers and students to work for social change. Received knowledge must be subjected to a critical analysis that uncovers its potential for reestablishing class, gender, and race barriers and conversely for building a more democratic social order. While those advocating a critical pedagogy differ in specific ideas about how curriculum and instructional practices should be constituted, they seem to be united in their objective to expose social and political injustice and in the process to play an active role in the development of critical and active citizens. The metaphor of the teacher as expert is rejected insofar as it suggests relationships that might disable students and teachers from being autonomous agents, from establishing their own efficacy in the world, and from working collectively to establish a more just and democratic social order.

Henry Giroux and the Transformative Intellectual

Henry Giroux is one of the most influential and controversial educators operating from within the critical tradition. Since the late 1970s his abundant writings have been a ferocious critique of traditional notions of schooling, as well as a complex attempt to provide a theoretical foundation for critical pedagogy. Much of Giroux's work has come at a time when conservative educational reforms have attempted to reestablish the basics at the core of the curriculum and to affirm the connection of schooling to economic issues. From Giroux's point of view, the dominant conservative discourse has signaled a retreat from acting on the moral and social purposes of schools and from viewing teaching as a political responsibility.[54] His attempt to reestablish a radical alternative must be understood, therefore, within a specific historical context. This includes a greater corporate influence in modern educational reform and a heightened tendency to view schools as agencies whose primary purpose is skill training and initiation into the dominant culture.

Giroux's first writings were tied to what has been termed the correspondence theory of schooling.[55] This theory closely mirrors the analysis above. Here schools are seen as largely conservative institutions that serve to perpetuate the prevailing economic order. Giroux praised this theory for challenging liberal and conservative views that the schools were unaffected by larger social pressures, but he soon saw that it also had many limitations. Foremost, it tended to be too deterministic. The correspondence theory emphasizes the connection between the values and dispositions taught by the school and those required of a compliant and servile workforce. Yet by focusing on compelling economic forces, Giroux argues, the theory pressupposes a monolithic view of domination and implies that students and teachers are passive creatures easily manipulated by outside pressures.[56] Such an analysis fails to account for the different political, social, and moral forces that influence educational institutions. More importantly, it posits such a closed account of institutional process that it handcuffs attempts at educational reform:

> Within its grimly mechanistic and overly-determined model of socialization there appears little room for developing a theory of schooling that takes seriously the notions of culture, resistance, and mediation. Even where contradictions and mediations are mentioned, they generally disappear under the crushing weight of capitalist domination. As such, these accounts are marred not only by a reductionist instrumentalism regarding the role and meaning of schools, but by a form of radical pesssimism that offers little hope for social change and even less reason for developing alternative educational practices.[57]

From Giroux's point of view, hopelessness and pessimism are especially grievous flaws when applied to educational concerns. Giroux strongly believes that schools are sites of political and social contestation where many times the poor and disenfranchised are denied educational opportunity. But the correspondence theory fails to recognize that teachers and students are not formed only by particular social and historical forces but can act on their environment to resist domination and eventually change conditions for the better. The point is critical for Giroux, who explicity and forcefully advocates a utopian mission for the schools. At the heart of Giroux's entire theoretical project lies the possibility that both teachers and students can become agents of social reform.

This project is founded on two important concepts that are particularly crucial for understanding the limits of expertise. The first revolves around knowledge. As many theorists have understood it, expertise is intimately connected to technology and to a mode of reasoning that Giroux and others describe as technical rationality. Here knowledge is viewed in neutral and objective terms. Having the merit of escaping subjective opinion and contested worldviews, knowledge seems universalized and scientific.[58] Its accumulation and transmission proceeds from specialized and credentialed experts who have established social credibility in part by adopting a language that emphasizes control, predictability, and efficiency. In this way, knowledge is valued primarily for instrumental purposes and lacks both a historical and social context. Expert solutions and expert analysis are seen to be applicable in a variety of settings and can be instituted from above without the direct participation and involvement of those who are its beneficiaries.

Giroux points out that this understanding of knowledge, which is rampant in the schools, teacher education institutions, and society at large, has particularly negative effects on intellectual life. On the one hand, it reduces teachers to the position of clerks or technicians whose management of instructional process is controlled by curriculum specialists.[59] On the other hand, it so removes students from the sources of knowledge and from reflecting on their own life situations as to render subject matter cold, vapid, and uninteresting.[60] Teachers, trained in programs that emphasize technical performance over moral and political investigation, lack, in Giroux's view, both the will and training to see themselves as curriculum makers or as moral and political agents who can act to create a more democratic learning environment.[61] Students, in turn, are not encouraged or taught to critically assess their own lived experiences or the knowledge of subject matter that is conveyed to them.

In this analysis, Giroux resembles many of the theorists we have already examined, particularly Counts, Dewey, and others in the social reconstructionist tradition. Giroux differs in his keen sensitivity to the idea of schools as contested sites, where decisions about curriculum and pedagogy reveal the relationship between knowledge and power and where such decisions usually tend to favor "that knowledge which provides formal justification for and legitimation of prevailing institutional arrangements."[62] Giroux points out that more is at stake than economic stratification. Rather, decisions about different ways of viewing the world are frequently sacrificed by an appeal to a "predetermined and hierarchically arrranged body of knowledge [which] is taken as the cultural currency to be dispensed to all children regardless of their differences and interests."[63] Within this view, cultural as well as technical knowledge is reduced to expertise and loses its subjective dimension. Giroux argues that such thinking hides the fact that knowledge is socially constructed and linked to human intentionality and behavior. It hides as well the fact that knowledge can be used as a form of social control—one way of positing a certain understanding of the world and preventing students from either questioning that view or exploring their own personal life histories.

At this point, the second construct underlying Giroux's theoretical position comes into play. It concerns the idea of voice and reflects, according to the analysis above, two interrelated notions of educational commitment. First, the sense that the differing experiences and backgrounds students bring to the classroom have the right to be articulated and examined. Second, the sense that education, as radically conceived, must be committed to a social vision grounded in radical pluralism and democracy. In Giroux's terms, the emphasis on voice depends not only on a recognition of schools as agents of social and political repression—what he terms the "language of critique"—but also on the hope and belief that schools are potential "democratic sites" open to the "language of possibility."

Giroux's criticism of many educational theorists flows from his concept of voice and this dual understanding of educational responsibility. For example, E. D. Hirsch and Allan Bloom received a great deal of attention in the late 1980s over their critique that the educational system was failing to inculcate those concepts and values that underlie the Western tradition. This critique reinforced the already well-grounded public perception that students in the United States were falling behind the accomplishments of students from other industrialized countries not only in math and the sciences but also in their understanding of literature, history, and geography. Giroux's response was that such a perception was a misunderstanding of the moral and political purposes of the schools to institute a more democratic social order.[64] It also represented a lack of understanding that the history of education was grounded in the explicit attempt to minimize and repress other voices, oppositional ways of understanding the world. Giroux argued that the "elitist" views of Hirsch and Bloom could, in fact, be summed up in a view of instruction that relied almost exclusively on 'transmission' and 'imposition.' By their understanding of cultural knowledge as fixed, objective, universal, and unproblematic, Hirsch and Bloom had made culture the stuff of expertise, material to be imposed upon students as received knowledge:

> The categories of meaning that students bring to the classroom and that provide them with a basis for producing and interpreting knowledge are simply denied by Bloom and Hirsch as viable categories of learning. Pedagogy, for both Bloom and Hirsch, is an afterthought. It is something one does to implement a preconstituted body of knowledge. The notion that pedagogy represents a method or technique for transmitting information, as well as an essential dynamic in the production and exchange of knowledge, necessitates that educators attend to the categories of meaning that students bring to the classrooom as well as to the fundamental question of why they should want to learn anything in the first place. This is an especially important consideration for those students in the public schools who know that the truth of their lives and experiences is omitted from the curriculum.[65]

Again, it is important to note Giroux's view that teachers and students must themselves learn the language of radical democracy and work for its fuller inception. This idea owes a great deal to Paulo Friere. It follows his advocacy of pedagogy as a political category and his criticism of the 'banking' theory of instruction in which knowledge is understood to be preformed, content simply to be 'deposited' into the empty vessels of student lives. Friere made clear how this trivialized and disempowered the meaning of student experience; Giroux makes even more clear how it misunderstands the role of teachers and the nature of instructional authority and power. In Giroux's view, authority cannot simply be derived from an unproblematic view of knowledge; it must be derived from the teacher's responsibility to "generate knowledge that presents concrete possibilities for empowering people."[66]

The concepts of authority and voice are, in this sense, connected to emancipation and the creation of a responsible and active citizenry. For this reason, Giroux rejects concepts of voice that seek to honor student experience and difference for their own sake. He makes clear that he advocates neither a vapid pluralism nor a type of relativism in which students are allowed merely to express their points of view apart from the responsibility to assess and interpret their legitimacy. For Giroux, the concept of voice is intimately connected to the commitment to democratic forms of life. Teachers have the responsibility to guide students to critically evaluate and analyse their own point of view, "to learn how not to be imprisoned by the worst dimensions of their sedimented histories and experiences."[67] Students also need to learn how to learn from different views of the world, "in order to critically appropriate the codes and vocabularies of others."[68] In any case, the need to attend to the different and varied lives of students does not liberate teachers from their responsibility to an education that serves self and social determination and an active democratic community. Both teachers and students are called to a type of intellectual rigor. Students have to acquire mastery of language as well as the capacity to think conceptually and critically. Teachers have to become:

> ...intellectuals in the technical sense, that is, attain a degree
> of mastery over the legacy of high culture as well as assimi-
> late and validate the elements of students' experience, which
> is intimately bound with popular culture.... The point is not
> to reproduce high culture; the point is to make these works
> part of our popular culture and eventually, on the basis of
> selection, eliminate their canonical status entirely.[69]

At this point, Giroux's conceptions of knowledge and voice merge in his representation of a teacher's work. He rejects the view that a teacher is an expert, either in the sense that a teacher's authority resides in technical skill or in an unassailable knowledge of cultural tradition. And he rejects the view that a teacher is a type of white-collar clerk, responsible only for carrying out the curriculum and instructional designs mandated by outside experts. Instead, he posits that a teacher's work is itself a form of 'intellectual labor,' a type of labor that demands the ability to think conceptually and critically.

Giroux calls such a teacher a transformative intellectual.[70] As unwieldy as this term might be, it is Giroux's attempt to recover the sense that an intellectual in any society has a particular social role, and the political sense that an intellectual in a democratic society must be explicitly involved in those modes of inquiry that support freedom, equality, and solidarity. In his view, a teacher is an intellectual in that her work is grounded in a quality of mind "characterized as having a creative, critical, and contemplative relationship to the world of ideas."[71] Teachers are also intellectuals in the sense that their social role obligates them to open up the possibility of inquiry to all kinds of people.[72]

Giroux recognizes that the category of intellectual can be misinterpreted. He is sensitive to those connotations of the term that promote elitist conceptions of knowledge and expertise and that, in the guise of an ideology of professionalism, serve to close off academic institutions from the wider community.[73] And he is particularly sensitive to the possibility of intellectualism being viewed apolitically, both in its retreat from immediate practical concerns and in its adherence to a view of nonpartisan, objective inquiry.[74] In contrast, Giroux posits a more inclusive view. Everyone is involved in intellectual life insofar as they mentally construct views of the world and thereby adopt a line of conduct that serves to sustain or modify a certain conception of the world. Teachers are intellectuals insofar as they are positioned institutionally and formally to help substantiate a certain view of social and political life. Intellectual partisanship is in this view unavoidable. Transformative intellectuals are unique in their understanding of the relationship between knowledge and power and in their partisan affirmation of forms of inquiry that support a more progressive social order.

Giroux's most recent writings have focused on ethics, public philosophy, and popular culture. On the one hand, this expands his interest in understanding the difference between education and schooling by seeking out how different cultural agencies, traditions, and personal biographies shape "political and moral expectations and locate us as moral beings."[75] On the other hand, it reflects a concern about how to account for an ethic and mode of behavior that best supports a public vision of the good life. Like Greene, Giroux recognizes the bankruptcy of a culture based upon consumerism and individualism. Yet it is not clear that radical educators have provided an alternative view. Giroux points to the paradox surrounding critical theory that relies on moral indignation and yet is fundamentally unable "to develop a moral and ethical discourse upon which to ground its own vision of society and schooling."[76] Without such a vision, critical educators lack any way to respond to the logic of self-interest and private morality that reduces concepts of citizenship to economic self-aggrandizement. For this reason, he notes, it is particularly important that teachers not find their sense of professionialism "through highly exclusionary and undemocratic appeals to knowledge and expertise." Teachers also cannot fall back on platitudes of liberal pluralism if they are to challenge and face the political nature of their work:

...teachers are bearers of critical knowledge, rules, and values through which they consciously articulate and problema-
tize their relationship to each other, to students, to subject
matter, and to the wider community. Such a view of authority
challenges the dominant view of teachers as primarily technicians or public servant, whose role is primarily to implement
rather than conceptualize pedagogical practice.... The concept of teacher as intellectual carries with it the imperative to
judge, critique, and reject those approaches to authority that
reinforce a technical and social divison of labor that silences
and disempowers both teachers and students.[77]

In this warning Giroux confronts once again two problems associated with expertise: first, the disposition to rely on a technical understanding of practice to the detriment of the moral and the political; second, the disposition to understand a division of labor that would
restrict public involvement to the province of the competent. He criticizes radical educators in this fashion as much as conservative thinkers.
If conservative educators all too often posit the stuff of schooling as
unproblematical, as if knowledge were certain and cultural production
were based on uniformity, radical educators tend to honor student differences as inherently sacred, as if the potential and limitation of personal experience did not have to be explored on the basis of how it
helped students engage a vision of democratic community and broader
collective hope.[78] In Giroux's view, teachers are under the obligation to
open up every aspect of formal education to active popular contestation. The idea that knowledge is power has in the crucible of modern
educational debate become commonplace. Giroux adds that knowledge
does more than distort reality; it also produces certain forms of life.
Within this dynamic, knowledge has a productive, positive function
and presents "concrete possibilities for empowering people."[79]

Conclusion

It should go without saying that the occupation of teaching now
requires more ability, more intelligence, more reserves of persistence
and competence than ever before. Postmodern theorists are fond of
pointing out the indeterminacy of a world in which the boundaries of
authority and knowledge have been dissolved. They point to the myri-
ad conversations that make up the human community and to both the
releases and restraints applied by dominant cultural forces as different

voices attempt to find their place within the social order. It does not take a surplus of imagination to think that this may describe today's typical classroom. Children's voices reveal many stories. In modern classrooms those stories tell not only of advantage and disadvantage, of ethnic clarity and cultural confusion, of poverty and affluence, but also of the need to construct a new vision of community, one to provide a fitting forum for the yet unspoken majesty of human potential.

It is easy to be taken aback by the responsibilities that this vision of the present and future places upon the resources of the average teacher. One does not find solace for these responsibilities within the language of many postmodern theorists, for it is a language built upon broad theoretical sweeps and upon the apocalyptic injunctions that descend from the perspective that the world has been turned upside down. Here it is helpful to pause occasionally to realize that underneath the postmodern appreciation of the import of the hour lies a typically modern arrogance and prejudice that no time has endured the pain of our own, that no age has so perched itself upon the edge of catastrophe. One does not find within many postmodern writers the disposition for self-effacement. Neither does one find that indispensable resource of any teacher, a sense of humor.

The prophetic language of both Maxine Greene and Henry Giroux shares the grandeur and sweep of postmodern writing. Perhaps because both are educators, one also finds a language of hope and a deep-seated and irradicable faith in the potential of students and teachers. More central to our concerns with expertise, one finds an appreciation and call for intelligence. Yet this sense of intellect stretches beyond a specialized, technical, and essentially private competence to include moral, social, and political sensibilities. It includes the ability to unlock the mysteries and mystifications behind privileged knowledge and to discover within the labyrinth of school bureaucracies those places where students and teachers can both face afresh the wonder and excitement of learning. Finally, it includes the creative courage to see oneself as an agent of progress and democratic citzenship, a creator rather than simply a dispenser of curriculum.

Greene and Giroux demand a great deal of the modern educator. Perhaps this is unavoidable since they are attempting to face what is surely one of the most difficult responsibilities affected by expertise, that of moral agency. Historically, expertise and moral agency have been allied within the province of professionalism. A professional was supposed to provide that ethical bridge between technical competence and service, the recognition that a client's vulnerability needed to be served not only by the expert's power, but also by his or her communal spirit. Such spirit is hard to sustain. Expertise, insofar as it constructs a world built upon the interrelated aspects of technical care and passive consumption, can erect social barriers to personal responsibility and to democratic imperatives for public judgment and action. The romantic answer to the excesses of expertise typically has involved the assertion of self-reliance and rugged individualism. Yet as the present age of self-involvement and the search for personal advantage has revealed, such answers can actually reassert those conditions and that social climate in which expertise thrives. In many ways, the expert as a social figure is nothing more than the consummate individual, that personage whose social status is primarily determined by an exclusive competence, marked as much by its removal from the broader cultural landscape as by its technical and specialized focus. Within the language of expertise itself resides little imperative for bridging the gap between the private world and the public, little warrant for balancing the appeal of personal reward with the social good.

Greene's contribution to this debate is to acknowledge the subtle distinction between the personal and the private. Teaching, she tells us, is a moral function, always explicitly bound up in ways of sense making and providing those spaces where others can make sense of their own lives. In this way, teaching and learning are always personal but never private. Teaching certainly engages our most private and intimate emotions and capacities, but it is also founded within the dialogical relations that make up our public selves. Unavoidably this entails reaching beyond ourselves into what Greene calls "intersubjective space." What this means for Greene is not always clear, but it certainly means the ability to understand other perspectives and, as she says, to be able "to become mindful, to share meanings, to conceptualize, and to make varied sense of lived worlds."[80] Typically for Greene, her insights into the public dimensions of life are not as sharp as those which reveal the range of obstacles. Thus, she notes that our public lives are bound up in the ability to create a social vision, the very lack of which creates another obstacle to personal freedom:

> When people cannot name alternatives, imagine a better state of things, share with others a project of change, they are likely to remain anchored or submerged, even as they proudly assert their autonomy. The same, paradoxically or not, is true when people uproot themselves, when they abandon families, take to the road, become strangers in desperate efforts to break loose from pre-established orders and controls.[81]

Giroux mirrors Greene's concern with the modern tendency to retreat into the private logic of self-interest, but he is even more concerned with the political and moral imperative to challenge prevailing forms of economic and social power. Moral agency for Giroux is bound up with the political, with the ability of teachers and students to see themselves as agents of change. At the heart of such a project is the democratic prospect and the concomitant need to work for social justice, empowerment, and solidarity. As with Greene, the precise elements of such work are not always explained. This can become annoying because Giroux's style is insistent and demanding. One is stirred by his rhetoric, but one also wants to know more. How, within the great diversity of American schools and within the divides that stretch across different ethnic, disadvantaged, and oppressed peoples, can one establish solidarity and the possibility for collective action? Giroux gives only general guides. He does point out that working progressively means forming alliances with community groups outside the school, opening up schools to "popular contestation," and engaging students in the critical analysis and dialogue that teaches the relation between knowledge and political power.

Foremost, Giroux wants to establish a new sense of instructional authority and an ethic that might reclaim for educators those senses of citizenship, character, and democratic activity not prone to chauvinism, nationalism, or forms of economic oppression. This effort provides one avenue for criticizing expertise. It attempts to honor an openness and spirit of inquiry that does not implicitly or explicitly limit discussion to procedural and technical concerns that seemingly have been stripped of all moral and social import. Here Giroux, without appealing to traditional or dominant sources of authority, still wants to claim for teachers that ethical foundation by which they might challenge and engage students in evaluating the strengths and weaknesses of different moral and cultural positions. He is quick to separate himself from the reluctance of some educators to impose upon students any moral direction. A sentimental respect of student difference, he writes, is "no excuse for the absence of any vision of the future."[82] Rather, despite the ambiguities inherent in a postmodern world:

> ...educators have a moral and ethical responsibility to develop a view of radical authority that legitimates forms of critical pedagogy aimed at both interpreting reality and transforming it. But what is at stake here is not just a struggle over authority and the production, distribution, and transformation of meaning, but also the equally important

task of changing those forms of economic and political power that promote human suffering and exploitation.[83]

This is heady business. While Giroux points out that the "political enormity of such a task is not meant to drive teachers to despair," it is impossible not to note that both his and Greene's conception of teacher commitment and responsibility is of heroic dimension. Such conceptions of the teacher—as stranger and as transformative intellectual—remind us of Dewey's thought that democracy must be won by every generation and that the obstacles to freedom and cooperative life must be confronted continually. In this sense, these two thinkers speak volumes on the sense of education that take as its focus the problems of public life itself. On the other hand, one always gets the sense that they really are directing themselves to a mature audience and that at times the struggles and forms of critical perception and activity they recommend fit the life of adults more than children.

The matter becomes significant as one begins to explore further the relation between education and the wider social and political context. Giroux quite rightly understands that curriculum and instruction are built upon political decisions, and for this reason he is fond of pointing out that the function of critical theory is to make the pedagogical political and the political pedagogical. On the other hand, it is quite another thing to bring all the contestation, the give-and-take of the political world into a classroom of the young. Such a view suggests social maturity when the character and perception of the young might not be wholly formed. It seems to suggest that the young are already autonomous individuals, prepared even at a young age to negotiate political and moral positions. Critical pedagogy centers on the need to begin with student experience and subject it as well as other aspects of received knowledge to interrogation. Yet one can engage and interrogate experience only when that experience is in place, and one can subject received traditions and values to analysis only when those traditions have been received. As C. A. Bowers has put the matter:

> Being told that one is a free and morally and rationally self-directing agent can be a heady message, particularly if it is learned at the stage of primary socialization when the initial world is being first constituted. Few students have the maturity or conceptual basis for questioning a cultural myth that, at the same time, enhances the sense of self.[84]

The point is critical. Especially in a world in moral and political disarray, it is appropriate to wonder about that foundation which might provide students with a moral sense and political purpose. Both Giroux and Greene in their appreciation of the problematic nature of knowledge and in their sensitivity to a "postmodern world that no longer has any firm boundaries," tend to discount the benefit of tradition. The past represents more a source of encumbrance than a resource to be utilized or a sense of history that deserves to be retained. But the concern for the foundational knowledge of children does not merely represent, as Giroux has responded, a "flight from serious politics and an apology for the status quo."[85] Rather, it represents the realization that as much as the school reflects political and social life, it does not simply reconstitute it. The school introduces the children to the world and prepares them for it by providing a secure place in which to grow. Tradition does not merely represent the burden of the customary or the legacy of historical oppression, it can also help form the community of memory that can be a foundation for cooperative spirit. It provides, in C. A. Bowers' words, those images of "humane relationships, cooperative life, and material and spiritual well being" that are not to be found in pedagogy of problem-solving or in critical reflection.[86]

Hannah Arendt has pointed out that at least in this sense—the sense of conservation—the school has a conservative mission.[87] It has a special relation to the past, as well as to authority and tradition, which is extremely different from the political. Conservatism, she notes, is the death of the political world. Since the world is always in a state of flux and will always be subject to the ruin of time, any effort to preserve the status quo only hinders those who might intervene to alter it and create it anew. In education, on the other hand, conservation means protecting and preserving the world from child and the child from the world. In that protection, the world itself is given the hope of preservation since the freshness that every generation brings bears the energy that prompts renewal.

Following Arendt, it seems fair to note that the "problem of education...lies in the fact that by its very nature it cannot forego authority or tradition, and yet must proceed in a world that is neither structured by authority nor held together by tradition."[88] In the postmodern world described by Greene and Giroux, this problem seems more critical than ever. The authority of the expert is strained by such a worldview since the very basis of a reasoned, objective knowledge is called into question. Yet it is also possible to imagine that the very ambiguity of contemporary life provides that atmosphere in which the comfort of technical, expert care seems all the more tempting. To raise the issue of the foundation of knowledge, especially moral and cultural knowledge, is to raise the issue of the ultimate sanction of instructional responsibility and of a teacher's justification for interfering in so many lives. How does one balance the need to teach those moral values that form a sense of cohesion in community life and those senses of structure that allow for pluralism and individual development? To Greene and Giroux's credit, this is precisely the question on which they have always been engaged. It is precisely the question the expert rarely faces.

Seven

Conclusion

The question of expertise raises enduring problems for our understanding of a teacher's practice. As this study has revealed, these problems are evident in the thought of many who have attempted to describe the role education is to play in the modern age. If H. G. Wells was correct that our times are in a race between education and disaster, then such considerations have implications well beyond the confines of a classroom.

It seems clear that in a technological age, experts are both unavoidable and needed. While some, like Ivan Illich, Myron Lieberman, and Milton Friedman, describe a world free of credentials and licensing requirements, the trust that many put in the competence of the expert needs to be honored by both training and skill. The teacher in particular seems duty-bound to honor that trust. One is reminded of the students of Socrates running to him because they were excited about the possibility of hearing the great teacher Protagoras.[1] Socrates cautioned them to consider what they were about to do. A person may go to a cobbler and at worst will wind up with a poor pair of shoes. A poor choice in tailors will yield the consumer only a bad suit of clothes. What mischief will a poor teacher do when the matter in question is the student's very soul?

In the bureaucratic corridors and peer-happy classrooms of the modern school, Socrates' lesson seems out of place. Still, the teachers in the studies conducted by Daniel Lortie and Philip Jackson pointed to moral issues when they described their reasons for teaching. Teaching success was determined less by a student's receiving high marks on a test than by the student's demonstrating characteristics that would make for a better person and a better citizen. For Lortie this represented in many ways an exercise in futility. What test can reveal the greater levels

of appreciation for literature, for art, or for one's democratic responsibilities? What objective measure can rate the self-esteem, the confidence,
and the dignity of a student who has not only learned to read but also
has learned that his skill might be used to help change the world and
make it a better place? Lacking an objective measure of that which they
most value, teachers could scarcely begin to claim that dimension of
ability befitting the expectations of the expert. Nonetheless, in the
descriptions of such students, teachers find not only their reason for
being, but also their awesome responsibilities to the larger public.

On what basis must such responsibilities be grounded? We have
looked at some answers to that question in the thought of educators
from Ellwood Cubberley to Henry Giroux, and the debate continues.
Many of the most recent studies of educational practice are even more
explicit in trying to base the professionalism of teachers on special technical competence, in particular through descriptions of the 'expert'
teacher in the classroom.[2] It is possible to consider such efforts as more
examples in a long line of research that began with the time–motion
studies of Frederick W. Taylor and then continued and expanded in the
work of W. W. Charters, Franklin Bobbitt, and Ralph Tyler. It is in
these kinds of studies that one still sees the idea of an objective rationality at work, though its employment is far more subtle. In the analysis
recently advanced by David Berliner, the intellectual qualities exhibited
by master teachers are deemed to be equivalent to the skill and vision
exhibited by experts generally, whether their fields be chess, surgery,
aviation, or athletics.[3] Berliner describes an instructional practice whose
intellectual demands are so strenuous as to be mastered only by the very
few. Novice and beginning practitioners are deemed to be in stages substantially removed from those of the technically proficient and expert.
For this reason he warns against amateur practitioners and recommends
more rigorous and structured training for those entering the craft. Character and moral sensitivity are neglected in favor of the pursuit of a
more specialized and arcane technical competence. The expertise
metaphor is enticing. If teachers are experts, then they will be able to
take their place among those exclusive groups whose extraordinary skill
and ability have earned them high social standing and credibility.

It would be simplistic to make light of such visions. While they
tend to advance the myth that the road to human betterment lies primarily within the domain of technical proficiency, they also have provided a powerful animus for social progress as well as for professional
advancement. What the myth neglects is the reality of the school itself
and the dynamics of the situation in which teacher and student behavior make sense. This is not to say that we cannot learn from others or

that the context in which everyone teaches is so idiosyncratic that each of us must rely on the existential virtues of pluck, courage, and good fortune to be successful. Stories and descriptions of good teaching tell us a great deal about the need to be prepared, to have in mind specific and understandable learning objectives, to gear method to content, and to expect the very best that students can offer. What they also tell us is that no one method can be successful in every instance and that even in the most well-prepared lesson, contingencies will arise that will subvert our best efforts. Indeed, what such descriptions tell us is that the vocabulary built around success and production is not the only language by which to describe effective teaching. Included as well must be qualities of perseverance, patience, humor, and good will.

The recent research into expertise has also yielded another most interesting finding. We now discover that even the most expert teachers lack the ability to describe exactly what they do in providing the opportunity for students to learn.[4] This matches what Jackson discovered in the inability of teachers to articulate with any degree of sophistication the basis for their classroom success. What Jackson attributed to environmental adjustment and Lortie attributed to technical stupidity, many now explain by the concept of 'tacit knowledge.' In fact, it is this concept that is used to describe the startling inability of experts in a variety of fields to explain the brilliant strategies which carried the moment. This observation reveals a new appreciation of the complexity of human understanding. Expertise appears to mean far more than having the right answers or formulating rules and principles to govern professional behavior. It refers to that sense of familiarity which, though grounded in experience and practice, appeals primarily to senses of intuition and 'feel.' Master teachers, as Maxine Greene once remarked, do indeed know so much more than they are ever able to relate. Knowledge, some theorists are given to say, is inextricably bound up in what it means to be human—in culture, in moral vision, and in the particular relationships that frame the learning event.[5]

Such an insight seems apt in the postmodern world that many thinkers now struggle to describe. As advances in computers and artificial intelligence have become more manifest, it has become important for philosophers to delineate with even more clarity those qualties of intellect that remain inextricably and unequivocally human.[6] Educators like Henry Giroux and Maxine Greene describe in exquisite detail the contingencies of a humanly constructed world and thus remind us that it has always been a mistake to separate human intellect from moral, social, and political vision. This insight is again substantiated by a wealth of new literature in which teachers describe their work.[7] Here knowledge appears to be less linear, less hierarchical, and less dependent on a detached and calculating rationality. Rather. knowledge is bound up in a teacher's sense of pedagogical mission, in his own biography, and in the special conditions under which he works. Jessica Howard, an elementary teacher, has recently described her place as a teacher as "being in the middle."[8] In her view, a teacher has the responsibility to provide spaces for the making of knowledge and to provide ways in which students might learn how "their own perspectives position them in the larger world." Unavoidably, this view of craft reflects a sense of knowledge that is both fluid and filled with social and moral expectation:

> Knowledge, in my view, means more than information; it carries notions of wholeness, expansiveness, and liveliness. The phrase 'pursuit of knowledge' suggests activity, relationship, and intimacy. You can't have knowledge without seeking.... Then, too, knowledge has an ethical or moral quality. As the pursuit of knowledge both broadens our connections to the world and deepens our awareness of our own questions, it also creates the possibility of increasingly responsible action.... I think of the pursuit of knowledge as requiring an inclusive, collaborative, open atmosphere. Thinking and speaking about our activities are critical to the forming and directing of the new impulses that lead us out again into the world, and thinking and speaking are public as well as private activities.[9]

The eloquence and sophistication of these kinds of reflections indicate, as John Goodlad has recently remarked, that education is a special profession, one whose standards of practice are not to be contained in the conventional appeals to detached reason and professional autonomy.[10] Perhaps for that reason it is helpful to reflect more deeply, as some have done, upon the fact that teaching has historically been the province of women.[11] In one view, this can be understood as a great burden, for not only has teaching fallen prey to a sexism that regards teaching as women's work and thus less significant than other work, but it also has created within the profession feelings of inferiority that always seem to lead to the search for more masculine and patriarchical senses of craft. It is important to note in this context that the great bulk of the reform efforts in teacher preparation and education generally is concerned with concepts of excellence that can be measured and tested and that can reassert hierarchical and competitive standards of accomplishment. Neither the Holmes Report nor the Carnegie Report for the

Advancement of Teaching mention seriously what Jane Martin Rich has called "the three C's of care, concern, and connection."[12] In this way are lost the fundamental insights that education is implicitly bound up with child rearing and that love and nurturance thus share as much in the instruction of children as the development of analytical reasoning or the imperatives of economic success.

To consider these matters seriously can lead us to far different images of teaching and learning than those reflected in the current reform imperatives. Feminist pedagogy depicts, for example, a very different type of classroom from the competitive and individualistic norm—one in which "people care about each other's learning as well as their own."[13] And recent research done on women's ways of knowing suggests the complexity of different modes of intellectual development.[14] Unavoidably, this points to new strengths in what formerly might have been considered pedagogical weaknesses. Thus, the ability to pose the appropriate questions and the ability to still one's own voice in an effort to draw out others seem crucial for human development. Qualities of discourse that formerly might have been considered tentative, vacillating, and diminutive become critical for the senses of 'connected knowing,' for the ability of teachers and students to accept and respond to the ambiguity and uncertainty that always attend genuine groping after knowledge.

Again, these matters are complex. The emphasis on moral and social development in learning becomes sentimental if placed over and above the cognitive demands of knowledge. The point should not be to emphasize one or the other, but to in some way strive for integration. In fact, it is easy to be staggered by the amount teachers need to know. And it is easy to see how this knowledge, which has grown considerably in the last twenty years, might be used to justify suggestions for requiring additional schooling and higher and more rigorous certification standards. One might talk about the moral basis of teaching, as Alan Tom, Henry Giroux and Maxine Greene have done in more than one way. The incompetent teacher, the teacher who has failed to master that minimum proficiency necessary to perform, has failed morally as well.

In some ways what most calls into question the argument for more standards, more credentials, and more specialty is not that it is incorrect, but that it is substantially correct, yet different implications can be drawn.[15] Jackson's and Tom's contention that we know very little about what produces learning lies not too far afield from the view that there is too much to know. In trying to understand and control the contingencies and forces that account for the complexity of human development, we perhaps become too confining and too restrictive of the mystery that makes these investigations a matter of such human and moral import in the first place. Questions of equity emerge as we find that more exclusive conceptions of professional practice limit severely the educational opportunities of the disadvantaged. Questions of ethics and social responsibility emerge as we consider once again George Counts' insight that regardless of effectiveness, educational questions always reflect back on the type of life we choose to live, the type of society we wish to engender.

On the practical level, the argument for extended teacher training carries with it the implication that more schooling will result in discernable benefits in the classroom. So far no studies reveal such a connection.[16] Also, the argument implies that extended training, which might disconnect liberal arts from professional course work, will allow teachers to incorporate more of the mass of knowledge needed to teach. This not only implies that such a mass of knowledge can be known in an objective way (in the same way, for example, as one might learn the facts about geography), but also suggests that *how* one learns has no necessary connection to *what* one learns.

Those who argue for teacher training in the context of a liberal arts university provide another argument.[17] They claim that the spirit of inquiry prevalent in such liberal arts training will better serve students who wish to teach and who must be learners themselves if they are to survive in the classroom. If there is simply too much to know, then it may be that what a teacher needs is not some measure of knowledge readily discernable by objective test, but an open attitude toward reflection, consideration, and pragmatic experimentation. It is just such an attitude that Dewey believed to be the most rewarding dimension of the scientific ethos, and it is this same attitude that is being stressed in another form by the modern advocates of critical pedagogy.

In the final analysis, the position of this work is that the perspectives of critical pedagogy and social reconstruction need to be taken far more seriously both within the schools and in the preparation of teachers. Critical pedagogy reminds us not only that the school represents a critical institution for cultivating capacities for self-discovery and fulfillment, but also that in a democratic society schools are of fundamental importance for cultivating those capacities of reflection, consideration, and responsibility upon which self-governance depends. Giroux's emphasis on the social injustices that education has played a role in fostering reminds us in a more *positive* light that schools and teachers have extraordinary power. If they are not the chief lever of social progress as the progressives believed, they are at least one institution in which the future is both fashioned and substantially called into being.

From the perspective of this book, the reconstructive power of the school places great demands upon the teacher. The notion of the teacher as transformative intellectual captures the social and political dimensions of this responsibility as well as the intellectual facilities required of the profession. One uses the term 'transformative intellectual' reluctantly because it adds another layer to the specialized languages that now so confuse and interrupt public discourse. On the other hand, in response to the appeal to expertise, the term indicates that intelligence has a public, active dimension and that it is unavoidably connected with political and social interests. For this reason alone it seems ludicrous to speak of education as an exclusive enterprise, one that must be left to the autonomous judgment of a specialized group.

This would suggest at the very least that the opportunity for different types of teacher training and schooling programs should not so easily be abandoned in the hope for a more uniform conception. It would suggest the importance of liberal arts to teacher preparation, which cannot afford to separate specialized training from the direct and meaningful consideration of the broader view. Finally, it would suggest that the question of the professional autonomy for the education profession has to be decided with a firm commitment to education as a public responsibility. Here one cannot so easily dismiss the 'loophole' of alternative certification on the basis that it lowers professional standards. One cannot easily dismiss the traditional right of parents in the United States to decide upon the form of education they believe is best for their own children, and one cannot forget the need of teachers to form alliances with the wider public if they are to construct an education that speaks to communal responsibilities.

Foremost is the importance of finding a language of compelling force for articulating our moral and political visions. Recent social criticism has made it clear how such a language has become lost in the clamor of a public discourse that stresses individualism and the pursuit of personal advantage.[18] It is important to recall that expertise itself relies on a vocabulary that stresses matters of efficiency, productivity, and control and that the conception of the teacher as an expert is itself a metaphor that carries with it certain public licenses and expectations.

We have argued that these expectations have as much to do with senses of communal belief and social relation as with displays of technical prowess. To conceive of the student as a client, the school as a service institution, or the teacher as an expert seems on the one hand to be only a manner of speaking. On the other hand, such language suggests that learning is a type of treatment and that schools themselves are the singular agencies meant to oversee the education of the young. To a large degree this is true, but as the romantics were particularly fond of pointing out, education is an activity that requires the participation of the student if it is to have meaning. If the romantics in their repugnance to authority identified only the most meager and malnourished role for the teacher, they reemphasized genuine distinctions between conditioning and indoctrination on the one hand and education on the other. Education implies freedom, personal responsibility over what one learns, and ownership of the knowledge one acquires. Education implicates the ability of the learner, not the ability of the teacher who has been able to manipulate events so as to promote the desired response in the subject. Even in the regimented and ordered institution of the school, as Waller long ago reminded us, the great charge of the teacher is to create a learning environment so that the personality of the learner himself will be engaged, and he will begin to participate more fully and integrally in the life of the democratic community.

In this sense, the service obligation of the professional educator seems not peripheral but central, and it seems inappropriate for it to be thrown into the shadow of increased technical competence. This conveys a central difference between the social relations governing the exchange between an expert and a layperson and the social relations that ideally exist between a teacher and student. Generally the epistemic authority of the teacher seems justified only as it 'self-destructs.' Usually the intervention of expert service leaves the reason and nature of client dependency untouched. The client remains in an unequal and subservient relationship; he has not developed the abilities to serve his own needs. By contrast, the teacher whose knowledge has not been used to make the student less dependent has failed. The point of educational service is to get the student to perform, not to reserve performance for the teacher.

It is possible that in this instance we have focused on the wrong question. We have considered whether the idea of the teacher as expert might be advantageous to the practice of teaching. We have not addressed whether teaching might be advantageous to the conception of expertise. It is no doubt too much to ask that doctors, lawyers, and those in other service professions adopt a wholly self-limiting concept of practice. Nonetheless, teachers have much to tell the world about the need to develop capacities for communication, for growth, and for sharing knowledge in the interest of a common good.

No doubt teachers too have much to learn about developing the types of institutional arrangements that make learning truly accessible to all elements of the population. Teachers will continue to be the special group most responsible for the education of the young; this seems unlikely to change in the foreseeable future. But many of the thinkers examined in this work have recommended limits. We must affirm that a public educational system built around exclusive knowledge and exclusive privilege operates at cross purposes. The practice of the teacher, no matter the amount of skill and knowledge involved, requires at the very least this unavoidable connection to both the wisdom and the needs of the common people. To keep that connection alive is critical for the teacher as well as for others who make a living by their special knowledge.

Notes

Chapter One. Introduction

1. Much of the recent use of the term "expert" has been in the literature of the social sciences and particularly psychology, which examines the different ways novices and skilled practitioners approach a similar problem. This literature has found its way into education just as reformers wish to increase the status of the teacher and assert professional autonomy. In this way, employing the metaphor of expertise is not simply scientific, it is political. See, for example, M. Chi, P. Feltovich, and R. Glaser, "Categorization and Representation of Physics Problems by Experts and Novices," *Cognitive Science* 5, no. 2 (1981): 121–52; David C. Berliner, "Ways of Thinking About Students and Classrooms by More and Less Experienced Teachers," in J. Calderhead, ed., *Exploring Teacher's Thinking* (London: Cassell Educational Limited, 1987), 60–83; and K. Carter et al., "Expert–novice Differences in Perceiving and Processing Visual Classroom Stimuli," in *Journal of Teacher Education* 39, no. 3 (1988): 25–31.

2. Daniel Bell, *The Coming of Post-Industrial Society* (New York: Basic Books, 1973).

3. Ibid., 174.

4. Ibid., 176.

5. Ibid.

6. John Kenneth Galbraith, *The New Industrial State* (New York: Signet Books, 1967), 408–409.

7. Thomas L. Haskell, "Introduction" in Thomas L. Haskell, ed., *The Authority of Experts* (Bloomington, Ind.: University of Indiana Press, 1984), xi.

8. Theodore Caplow, *The Sociology of Work* (New York: McGraw-Hill, 1964), 23.

9. Bell, *The Coming of Post-Industrial Society,* 179.

10. Caplow points out that the very word "mistery," originally referred to membership in a craft guild and the types of secret understandings such membership implied. Now, he notes, "the mutual incomprehensibility of occupational languages, the increasingly rigid organization of occupational interest groups, and the barrier between working environments combine to create a situation for which there is no close historic parallel, when habits, customs and standards of a neighbor's occupational world may be no more familiar than those of the Australian aborigines." See Caplow, *The Sociology of Work,* 23.

11. Ibid.

12. Robert Marquand, "National Education Conference Focuses on 'Technological Literacy' in the U.S.," *Christian Science Monitor* 78, no. 60 (February 21, 1986): 21–22.

13. "Proportion of 'Scientifically Literate' U.S. Adults Is Less Than 6 Percent, According to New Study," *Education Week* 8, no. 18 (January, 25, 1989): 25.

14. C. S. Lewis, *Abolition of Man* (London: Oxford University Press, 1944), 26.

15. Stephen P. Stich and Richard E. Nisbett, "Expertise, Justification and the Psychology of Inductive Reasoning," in Thomas L. Haskell, ed., *The Authority of Experts* (Bloomington: Indiana University Press, 1984), 226–41.

16. Ibid., 237.

17. See Frank Fischer, *Technocracy and the Politics of Expertise* (Newbury Park, Calif.: Sage Publications, 1990); Langdon Winner, *Autonomous Technology: Technics-Out-Of-Control as a Theme in Political Thought* (Cambridge, Mass.: M.I.T. Press, 1977; Ralph E. Lapp, *The New Priesthood: The Scientific Elite and the Uses of Power* (New York: Harper and Row, 1965); B. Bruce-Briggs, ed., *The New Class?* (New Brunswick, N. J.: Transaction Books, 1979); and Jethro K. Lieberman, *The Tryanny of the Experts* (New York: Walker and Company, 1970).

18. Zbigniew Brzezinski, "The Technetronic Society," *Encounter* 30, no. 1 (January, 1968): 16–26. For a more recent exposition see Anthony Lukas, "Harvard's Kennedy School: Is Competence Enough?" *The New York Times Magazine* (March 12, 1989): 36.

19. See William E. Akin, *Technocracy and the American Dream* (Berkeley: University of California Press, 1977).

20. See Eliot Freidson, *Profession of Medicine* (New York: Dodd, Meade, and Company, 1972); Ivan Illich, *Medical Nemesis* (New York: Pantheon Books, 1976); and Irving Kenneth Zola, "Healthism and Disabling Medical-

ization," in Ivan Illich et al., *Disabling Professions* (Boston: Marion Boyars, 1979), 41–67.

21. Illich, *Medical Nemesis*, 15–22.

22. Norman Cousins, *Anatomy of an Illness as Perceived by the Patient* (New York: W.W. Norton, 1979).

23. Susan Sontag, *Illness as Metaphor* (New York: Farrar, Straus and Giroux, 1978).

24. Thomas Haskell, "Preface," in *The Authority of Experts*, xiii.

25. Karen S. Edwards, "The Malpractice Crisis: A National Perspective," *The Ohio State Medical Journal* 82, no. 9 (September, 1986): 641–45.

26. Statistics cited in Joel Spring, *American Education: An Introduction to Social and Political Aspects* (New York: Longman, 1991), 42.

27. *Digest of Educational Statistics, 1988* (Washington, D.C.: U.S. Government Printing Office, 1988), 77.

28. Spring, *American Education, 42.*

29. Stephen T. Kerr, "Teacher Specialization and the Growth of a Bureaucratic Profession," in *Teachers College Record* 84, no. 3 (Spring, 1983): 630.

30. Ibid., 631.

31. *Digest of Educational Statistics,* 58.

32. Kerr, "Teacher Specialization," 631–34.

33. Ibid., 633.

34. The National Commission for Excellence in Education, *A Nation at Risk, the Full Account* (Cambridge, Mass.: USA Research, 1984), 5.

35. The Holmes Group, *Tomorrow's Teachers* (East Lansing, Mich.: The Holmes Group, 1986); and The Carnegie Forum on Education and the Economy, *A Nation Prepared: Teachers for the 21st Century* (New York: Carnegie Corporation, 1986).

36. For summaries of the recommendations of the two reports, see The Holmes Group, *Tomorrow's Teachers,* 4; and The Carnegie Forum on Education and the Economy, *A Nation Prepared,* 3.

37. Lynn Olson, "Holmes Group Finds Mixed Results in Universities First Reform Efforts," *Education Week* 8, no. 20 (February 8, 1989).

38. One critical issue facing the board is whether to concentrate on assessment as the sole method of certification or also to require that board-

certified teachers complete approved programs for certification. See Ann Bradley, "Teaching Board Says Professional Degree Not Required," *Education Week* 8, no. 40 (August 2, 1989).

39. The medical metaphor is an explicit part of both reports, occurring in reference to the greater status and pay of doctors as well as to the "clinical" studies and school sites that would act like "teaching hospitals." The Holmes Report, with its added emphasis on the professionalization process, is more explicit about the metaphor. The Carnegie Report follows *A Nation at Risk* in connecting economic decline with poor performance in school. This emphasis mutes somewhat the medical metaphor, but it cannot be forgotten that the Carnegie Foundation funded the report by Abraham Flexner that led to the reform of medical education. For explicit references, see The Holmes Group, *Tomorrow's Teachers*, 8, 12, 56, 67; and The Carnegie Forum on Education and the Economy, *A Nation Prepared*, 7, 58, 76.

40. This view is consistent with the ideas of scientific management expressed by Fredrick Taylor. For a good analysis of the effect and reach of such ideas, see Samuel Haber, *Efficiency and Uplift* (Chicago: University of Chicago Press, 1964).

41. Wendy Carlton, *"In Our Professional Opinion...": The Primacy of Clinical Judgement Over Professional Skills* (Notre Dame, Ind.: University of Notre Dame Press, 1978).

42. See Raymond Callahan, *Education and the Cult of Efficiency* (Chicago: University of Chicago Press, 1962); Randall Collins, *The Credential Society: An Historical Sociology of Education and Stratification* (New York: Academic Press, 1979); and David Tyack and Elisabeth Hansot, *Managers of Virtue: Public School Leadership in America, 1820–1980* (New York: Basic Books, 1982).

Chapter Two. Expertise in Progressive Thought

1. Thomas L. Haskell, ed., *The Authority of Experts* (Bloomington: Indiana University Press, 1984).

2. Quoted in Howard P. Segal, *Technological Utopianism in American Culture* (Chicago: University of Chicago Press, 1985), 29.

3. Harold L. Wilensky, "The Professionalization of Everyone?," *American Journal of Sociology* 70, no. 2 (September 1964): 53–79.

4. Burton J. Bledstein, *The Culture of Professionalism* (New York: W. W. Norton, 1976), 53–79.

5. Ibid., 326–27.

6. David Tyack and Elisabeth Hansot, *Managers of Virtue* (New York: Basic Books, 1982), 44–56.

7. Merle L. Borrowman, *Teacher Education in America* (New York: Teachers College Press, 1965), 24–25.

8. Joel Spring, *The American School 1642–1985* (New York: Longman, 1986), 112–32.

9. Edward L. Thorndike, "The Psychology of the Half-Educated Man," *Harpers Monthly Magazine* 40 (April, 1920): 666–70.

10. Tyack and Hansot, *Managers of Virtue*, 114–15.

11. John Dewey, "My Pedagogical Creed," *School Journal* 54 (January, 1897): 17.

12. Tyack and Hansot, *Managers of Virtue*, 105–14.

13. Samuel Haber, *Efficiency and Uplift* (Chicago: University of Chicago Press, 1964), xi.

14. Jesse B. Sears and Adin D. Henderson, *Cubberley of Stanford* (Stanford: Stanford University Press, 1957), 63.

15. I am indebted in this discussion to the analysis of Tyack and Hansot, *Managers of Virtue*, 121–28.

16. Quoted in Sears and Henderson, *Cubberley of Stanford*, 33.

17. Lawrence A. Cremin, *The Transformation of the School* (New York: Alfred A. Knopf, 1961), 67–68.

18. Many historians have indulged in this complaint against Cubberley, but see especially Lawrence A. Cremin, *The Wonderful World of Ellwood Patterson Cubberley* (New York: Bureau of Publications, Teachers College, Columbia University, 1965); Michael B. Katz, "Education and Social Development in the Nineteenth Century," in Paul Nash, ed., *History and Education* (New York: Random House, 1970), 83–119; Bernard Bailyn, *Education in the Forming of American Society* (Chapel Hill: University of North Carolina Press, 1960).

19. George E. Arnstein, "Cubberley: The Wizard of Stanford," *History of Education Journal* 5, (Spring, 1954): 73–81.

20. Cremin, *The Wonderful World of Ellwood Patterson Cubberley*, 4.

21. Ellwood P. Cubberley, *Public School Administration* (Boston: Houghton Mifflin, 1922), 201.

22. Ibid., 176–78.

23. Ibid., 196–97.

24. Quoted in David Tyack, "Governance and Goals: Historical Perspectives in Education," in Don Davies, ed., *Communities and Their Schools* (New York: McGraw-Hill, 1981), 19.

25. Ellwood P. Cubberley, *Changing Conceptions of Education* (Boston: Houghton Mifflin, 1909), 14–15.

26. For a fuller explanation of the network process, see Tyack and Hansot, *Managers of Virtue*, 140–41.

27. Quoted in Ibid., 141.

28. Quoted in Ibid., 140.

29. Arnstein, "Cubberley: The Wizard of Stanford," 73–81.

30. Cubberley, *Public School Administration*, 222–24.

31. Cubberley, *Changing Conceptions of Education*, 63.

32. Ibid., 56–57.

33. Quoted in Tyack and Hansot, *Managers of Virtue*, 127.

34. William E. Akin, *Technocracy and the American Dream* (Berkeley: University of California Press, 1977).

35. For a discussion of how this process might work today in such matters as thinking skills and learning styles, see Catherine Cornbleth, "The Persistence of Myth in Teacher Education," in Thomas S. Popkewitz, ed., *Critical Studies in Education* (London: Falmer Press, 1987).

36. William James, *Talks to Teachers on Psychology and to Students on Some of Life's Ideals* (New York: Henry Holt and Company, 1912), 4, 9.

37. John Dewey, *Sources of a Science of Education* (New York: Horace Liveright, 1929), 13.

38. Ibid., 15–16.

39. A good background on the origins and thought of the social reconstructionists is provided by C. A. Bowers, *The Progressive Educator and the Depression* (New York: Random House, 1969).

40. Quoted in Lawrence J. Dennis, *George S. Counts and Charles A. Beard: Collaborators for Change* (Albany: State University of New York Press, 1989), 78.

41. George S. Counts, *The Social Foundations of Education* (New York: Charles Scribner's Sons, 1934), 9.

42. For a discussion of Counts' early works, see Gerald L. Gutek, *The Educational Theory of George S. Counts* (Columbus: The Ohio State University Press, 1970), 17–47.

43. George S. Counts, *The Social Composition of Boards of Education* (Chicago: University of Chicago Press, 1927), 83–90.

44. Ibid., 90.

45. Counts, *The Social Foundations of Education*, 559.

46. Ibid., 558–59.

47. Lawrence J. Dennis and William Edward Eaton, eds., *George S. Counts: Educator for a New Age* (Carbondale: Southern Illinois University Press, 1980), 3.

48. Counts, *The Social Foundations of Education*, 75–76. See also Gutek, *The Educational Theory of George S. Counts*, 89–114.

49. For a full discussion of the issue of indoctrination see Gutek, *The Educational Theory of George S. Counts*, 115–34; and Bowers, *The Progressive Educator and the Depression*, 3–45.

50. George S. Counts, *Dare the School Build a New Social Order* (New York: John Day Company, 1932), 9–10.

51. Ibid., 13–27.

52. Bowers, *The Progressive Educator and the Depression*, 17–18.

53. See in particular the response of Henry W. Holmes, "The Teacher in Politics," *Progressive Education* 9 (1932): 414.

54. This became even more important with the rise of fascist and Nazi movements in Europe. See George S. Counts, *The Schools Can Teach Democracy* (New York: John Day Company, 1939), 5–14.

55. George S. Counts, *Decision Making and American Values in School Administration* (New York: Bureau of Publications, Teachers College, Columbia University, 1954), 6.

56. Raymond A. Callahan, *Education and the Cult of Efficiency* (Chicago: University of Chicago Press, 1962). This remains the seminal criticism and history of the efficiency movement in education, yet it is interesting to note how even Callahan's writing follows the problem/solution mode of thought that also drove the early progressives. Ironically, nowhere is this more in evidence than in the writing of Counts, who was one of the biggest critics of the efficiency experts. Counts frequently prefaces his calls to action with the most vivid descriptions of the current social crisis.

57. Eliot Freidson, *Patients' Views of Medical Practice* (New York: Russell Sage Foundation, 1961) 197–202.

58. Cremin, *Transformation of the School*, 184.

59. For a good, insightful discussion of Addams' educational ideas, see Lawrence A. Cremin, *American Education: The Metropolitan Experience, 1876–1980*

(New York: Harper and Row, 1988), 174–79; and the introductory essay by Ellen Condliffe Lagemann in Ellen Condliffe Lagemann, ed., *Jane Addams on Education* (New York: Teachers College Press, 1985), 1–39. Much of the account that follows is owed to these works.

60. Christopher Lasch, *The Social Thought of Jane Addams* (Indianapolis: Bobbs-Merrill Co., 1965), xiv.

61. Jane Addams, "Widening the Circle of Enlightenment: Hull House and Education," in Lagemann, ed., *Jane Addams on Education*, 211.

62. Cremin, *American Education*, 175.

63. Quoted in Ibid., 176.

64. Roy Lubove, *The Professional Altruist: The Emergence of Social Work as a Career* (Cambridge: Harvard University Press, 1965), 104.

65. Ibid.,158.

66. Cremin, *American Education*, 79.

67. Jane Addams, "A Function of the Social Settlement," *Annals of the American Academy of Political and Social Science* 13 (1899): 339–40.

68. Lagemann, ed., *Jane Addams on Education*, 35.

69. Lubove, *The Professional Altruist*, 23.

70. Lasch, ed., *The Social Thought of Jane Addams*, xiv.

Chapter Three. Moral Authority and Technical Competence

1. Edward Eggleston, *The Hoosier Schoolmaster* (New York: Grosset and Dunlap, 1889), 37,39.

2. Ernest L. Boyer, *High School: A Report on Secondary Education in America* (New York: Harper and Row, 1983), 154–60.

3. See especially Theodore Sizer, *Horace's Compromise: The Dilemma of the American High School* (Boston: Houghton Mifflin, 1984); John I. Goodlad, *A Place Called School* (New York: McGraw-Hill, 1984); Robert L. Hampel, *The Last Little Citadel* (Boston: Houghton Mifflin, 1986); Ken Macrorie, *20 Teachers* (New York: Oxford University Press, 1984); Larry Cuban, *How Teachers Taught* (New York: Longman, 1984); and Philip Jackson, *The Practice of Teaching* (New York: Teachers College Press, 1986).

4. See especially The Holmes Group, *Tomorrow's Teachers* (East Lansing, Mich., The Holmes Group, 1986); and The Carnegie Forum on Education and the Economy, *A Nation Prepared: Teachers for the 21st Century* (New York: The Carnegie Corporation, 1986).

5. Willard S. Elsbree, *The American Teacher* (New York: American Book Company, 1939), 395–426.

6. David B. Tyack, *The One Best System* (Cambridge: Harvard University Press, 1974), 208.

7. Ibid., 207.

8. Ibid., 210.

9. George S. Counts, *The Selective Character of American Secondary Education* (Chicago: University of Chicago, 1922), 153–56.

10. Lawrence A. Cremin, *The Transformation of the School* (New York: Alfred A. Knopf, 1961), 190.

11. Ibid.

12. Tyack, *One Best System*, 215.

13. Ibid., 208–14. See also Stephen Jay Gould, *The Mismeasure of Man* (New York: W.W. Norton, 1981).

14. Tyack, *One Best System*, 214.

15. Burton J. Bledstein, *The Culture of Professionalism* (New York: W.W. Norton, 1976), 80–128.

16. Eliot Freidson, *Profession of Medicine* (New York: Dodd, Meade and Company, 1972), 6–12.

17. For a celebration of the evolution of medicine as a profession based on science see Richard Shryock, *The Development of Modern Medicine* (Baltimore: Johns Hopkins University Press, 1966).

18. Quoted in Ibid., 262.

19. Some research has pointed out that doctors begin their practice with ethical and interpersonal considerations being foremost in their understanding of professional competence. But soon the bureaucratic nature of hospital practice, the pressure to keep up with technical developments, and the high expectations of their patients point them to a more technical orientation. See Wendy Carlton, *"In Our Professional Opinion...": The Primacy of Clinical Judgement over Professional Skills* (Notre Dame, Ind.: University of Notre Dame Press, 1978).

20. Magali Sarfetti Larson, *The Rise of Professionalism* (Berkeley: University of California Press, 1977), 22.

21. Bledstein, *The Culture of Professionalism*, 287–300.

22. Elsbree, *The American Teacher*, 192–98.

23. Ibid., 499–510.

24. Joel Spring, *The American School 1642–1985* (New York: Longman, 1986), 249–52.

25. Statistics cited in David Tyack and Elisabeth Hansot, *Managers of Virtue* (New York: Basic Books, 1982), 154.

26. Raymond E. Callahan, *Education and the Cult of Efficiency* (Chicago: University of Chicago Press, 1962).

27. Elsbree, *The American Teacher*, 199–208.

28. Ibid., 428.

29. Spring, *The American School 1642–1985*, 136–38.

30. Abraham Flexner, *Medical Education in the United States and Canada* (New York: Carnegie Foundation, Bulletin no. 4, 1910). For a discussion of the repercussions of the Flexner report, see Larson, *The Rise of Professionalism*, 161–66.

31. Abraham Flexner, *Universities: American, English, German* (Oxford: Oxford University Press, 1930), 96–103.

32. Willard Waller, *The Sociology of Teaching* (New York: John Wiley and Sons, 1932).

33. The recognition of Waller as a noted sociologist has receded over the years, yet according to William J. Goode and colleagues, he continues to be "discovered" occasionally by admiring scholars. For a penetrating character study of Waller, see William J. Goode, Frank F. Furstenberg, Jr., and Larry R. Mitchell, eds., *Willard Waller: On the Family, Education, and War* (Chicago: University of Chicago Press, 1970), 1–110.

34. Ibid., 53–54.

35. Waller, *The Sociology of Teaching*, 30.

36. Ibid., 28.

37. Ibid., 49.

38. Ibid., 63–66.

39. Ibid., 34.

40. Ibid., 40–41.

41. Ibid., 45.

42. Ibid., 375.

43. Ibid., 59–60.

44. Ibid., 378.

45. Ibid., 49–66.

46. Ibid., 64.

47. Goode, Furstenberg, and Mitchell, *Willard Waller: On the Family, Education, and War,* 84.

48. Waller, *The Sociology of Teaching,* 441.

49. Ibid., 391.

50. Ibid., 444–45.

51. Ibid., 444.

52. Ibid., 454.

53. Gary D. Fenstermacher, "Educational Accountability: Features of the Concept," *Theory Into Practice* 18, no. 5 (December, 1979): 330.

54. Statistics quoted in Joel Spring, *American Education: An Introduction to Social and Political Aspects* (New York: Longman, 1991), 43.

55. John I. Goodlad, "An Ecological Version of Accountability," *Theory Into Practice* 18, no. 5 (December, 1979): 308.

56. C. A. Bowers, "The Ideological-Historical Context of an Educational Metaphor," *Theory Into Practice* 18, no. 5 (December, 1979): 316–22.

57. Daniel C. Lortie, *Schoolteacher: A Sociological Study* (Chicago: University of Chicago Press, 1975).

58. Ibid., 214–44.

59. See especially Daniel C. Lortie, "Laymen to Lawmen: Law School, Careers, and Socialization," *Harvard Educational Review* 29, no. 4 (Fall, 1959): 352–59; ———, "The Teacher's Shame: Anger and the Normative Commitments of Classroom Teachers," *School Review* 75, no. 2 (Summer, 1967): 155–71; and ———, "The Balance of Control and Autonomy in Elementary School Teaching," in Amitai Etzioni, ed., *The Semi-Professions and Their Organization* (New York: Free Press, 1969), 1–53.

60. Terence J. Power, *Professions and Power* (London: Macmillan, 1972), 23–30.

61. Amitai Etzioni, "Preface" in Amitai Etzioni, ed., *The Semi-Professions and Their Organization* (New York: Free Press, 1969), viii.

62. William J. Goode, "The Theoretical Limits of Professionalization," in Amitai Etzioni, ed., *The Semi-Professions and Their Organization* (New York: Free Press, 1969), 295–97.

63. Harold L. Wilensky, "The Professionalization of Everyone?," *The American Journal of Sociology* 70, no. 2 (September, 1964): 137–58.

64. Lortie, *Schoolteacher,* viii.

65. Other thinkers have commented critically on Waller's fall from respectability. See Christopher Lasch, *Haven in a Heartless World* (New York: Basic Books, 1977), 50–55.

66. Lortie, *Schoolteacher,* 22.

67. Ibid., 17–18.

68. Ibid., 39.

69. Ibid., 41.

70. Ibid., 53–54.

71. Ibid.

72. Ibid., 67–81.

73. Ibid., 39–40, 76–79, 133.

74. Ibid., 79.

75. Ibid., 181–86.

76. Ibid., 99–100.

77. Ibid., 184.

78. Ibid., 109–32.

79. Ibid., 159–60.

80. Ibid., 136.

81. Ibid., 222.

82. Most reviewers were very favorable to Lortie's positions. See especially Ronald G. Corwin, *Social Forces* 54 (June, 1976): 948; and Elizabeth G. Cohen, *American Journal of Sociology* 81 (March, 1976): 1226. Corwin does criticize Lortie for his failure to appreciate the differences between teaching and other occupations. Cohen remarks that Lortie's recommendations on the selective recruitment of teachers are worrisome because they imply some sort of ideological test.

83. Joseph Featherstone, *What Schools Can Do* (New York: Liveright, 1976), 160.

84. Philip W. Jackson, *Life in Classrooms* (New York: Holt, Rinehart, and Winston, 1968), 163–69.

85. Ibid., 167.

86. Thomas L. Haskell, "Professionalism Versus Capitalism: R. H. Tawney, Emile Durkheim, and C. S. Peirce on the Disinterestedness of Professional Communities," in Thomas L. Haskell, ed., *The Authority of Experts* (Bloomington: Indiana University Press, 1984), 180–225.

Chapter Four: The Teacher as Expert Authority

1. Normand R. Bernier and Jack E. Williams, *Beyond Belief: Ideological Foundations of American Education* (Englewood Cliffs, N. J.: Prentice-Hall, 1973), 158–62.

2. Merle Curti, "Intellectuals and Other People," *American Historical Review* 60 (January, 1955): 259–82.

3. John F. Kasson, *Civilizing the Machine: Technology and Republican Values in America*, 1776–1900 (New York: Viking Press, 1976), 16–17.

4. For a delightful exposition of this debate, see Robert Pirsig, *Zen and the Art of Motorcycle Maintenance* (New York: Bantam Books, 1974), 60–72.

5. Bernier and Williams, *Beyond Belief*, 169–74.

6. Ralph Waldo Emerson, *Selected Prose and Poetry* (New York: Holt, Rinehart and Winston, 1950), 168.

7. Richard Hofstadter, *Anti-intellectualism in American Life* (New York: Alfred A. Knopf, 1964), 362–68.

8. Theodore Roszak, *Making of a Counter Culture* (New York: Doubleday and Company, 1968), xiii.

9. Ibid., 7.

10. See especially Paul Goodman, *Growing Up Absurd* (New York: Vintage Books, 1960); and ———, *Compulsory Mis-education and the Community of Scholars* (New York: Vintage Books, 1964).

11. Goodman, *Compulsory Mis-education and the Community of Scholars*, 8–12.

12. For a discussion of this point, see Henry J. Perkinson, *Two Hundred Years of American Educational Thought* (New York: David McKay Company, 1976), 284.

13. Goodman, *Growing Up Absurd*, 12.

14. Goodman, *Compulsory Mis-education and the Community of Scholars*, 61.

15. Ibid., 87.

16. Goodman paricularly notes the article by Lauren Resnick, "Programmed Instruction of Compex Skills," *Harvard Educational Review* 33, no. 3 (Fall, 1963): 439–71.

17. Goodman, *Compulsory Mis-education and the Community of Scholars*, 87.

18. Ibid., 86.

19. Ibid., 90.

20. Ibid., 87–88.

21. Edgar Z. Friedenberg, *The Vanishing Adolescent* (New York: Dell Publishing, 1959), 17.

22. Ibid., 32–35.

23. Perkinson, *Two Hundred Years of Educational Thought*, 289.

24. Friedenberg, *The Vanishing Adolescent*, 92–95.

25. Ibid., 91, 133–38.

26. Edgar Z. Friedenberg, *Coming of Age in America* (New York: Random House, 1965), 250.

27. Jonathan Kozol, *Death at an Early Age: The Destruction of the Hearts and Minds of Negro Children in the Boston Public Schools* (Boston: Houghton Mifflin, 1967).

28. Ibid., 111–12. Most notable to Kozol was not only the explicitly racist and sometimes violent actions of his peers, but also the advice for the teacher not to become involved with students in any personal way.

29. Herbert Kohl, *36 Children* (New York: New American Library, 1967).

30. Ibid., 24.

31. Ibid., 29.

32. Ibid., 26.

33. Ibid., 42.

34. Ibid., 52.

35. John Holt, *How Children Fail* (New York: Delacorte Press, 1982), 145.

36. Ibid., 145–46.

37. Ibid., 189.

38. Ibid., 26–27.

39. Ibid., 34.

40. Ibid., 162.

41. Ibid., 162.

42. Ibid., 109.

43. For a brief biographical sketch of Illich as well as a good analysis of his work and the work of Paulo Friere, see John L. Elias, *Conscientization and Deschooling* (Philadelphia: The Westminster Press, 1976).

44. Ivan Illich, *Deschooling Society* (New York: Harper and Row, 1971).

45. Ibid., 10, 29.

46. Ibid., 26–28.

47. Ibid., 49–51.

48. Ivan Illich, "Disabling Professions," in Ivan Illich, et al., *Disabling Professions* (Boston: Marion Boyars, 1979), 16–19.

49. Illich, *Deschooling Society*, 6–9.

50. Ibid., 12–13.

51. Ibid., 26–30.

52. Bernier and Williams, *Beyond Belief*, 160.

53. Ivan Illich, *Medical Nemesis* (New York: Pantheon Books, 1976), 40–43.

54. Illich, *Deschooling Society*, 75–77.

55. Ibid., 83–85.

56. Ibid., 105–15.

57. This point is made by Cremin in comparing the American education situation with that of Germany under Adolph Hitler and with that of the Soviet Union under Joseph Stalin. See Lawrence A. Cremin, *The Genius of American Education* (New York: Vintage Books, 1965), 15–17.

58. Quoted in Perkinson, *Two Hundred Years of American Educational Thought*, 300.

59. Jonathan Kozol, *The Night Is Dark and I Am Far from Home* (Boston: Houghton Mifflin, 1975), 95–105.

60. Ibid., 114.

61. Quoted in Perkinson, *Two Hundred Years of American Educational Thought*, 299.

62. See Donald A. Schon, *The Reflective Practitioner* (New York: Basic Books, 1983); and Charles Derber, ed., *Professionals as Workers: Mental Labor in Advanced Capitalism* (Boston: G.K. Hall and Company, 1982).

63. Neil Postman, "My Ivan Illich Problem," in Alan Gartner, Colin Greer, and Frank Riessman, eds., *After Deschooling, What?* (New York: Harper and Row, 1973), 137–47.

64. Arthur Pearl, "The Case for Schooling America," in Gartner et al., eds., *After Deschooling, What?*, 112–17.

65. For a description of "negative freedom," see Isaiah Berlin, *Four Essays on Liberty* (New York: Oxford University Press, 1970), 118–72.

66. This line of argument has been pursued particularly by Perkinson. See Henry J. Perkinson, *The Possibilities of Error* (New York: David McKay Company, 1971); and Ronald M. Swartz, Henry J. Perkinson, and Stephenie G. Edgerton, eds., *Knowledge and Fallibilism: Essays on Improving Education* (New York: New York University Press, 1980).

67. Milton J. Friedman, *Capitalism and Freedom* (Chicago: University of Chicago Press, 1962).

68. See Myron Lieberman, *Beyond Public Education* (New York: Praeger Publishers, 1986). Lieberman's career has undergone several changes. In the 1950s, he was a strong proponent of teacher unions and collective bargaining. He also argued that education reform depended on the development of a strong educational elite. More recently he has opposed collective bargaining and has argued that unions do not represent the best interests of teachers or of education. Like Friedman, he now seems to argue for more market control of education as a way of eliminating incompetence and insuring accountability. His initial opinions in support of unions were delivered in Myron Lieberman, *Education as a Profession* (Englewood Cliffs, N. J.: Prentice-Hall, 1956); and ————, *The Future of Public Education* (Chicago: University of Chicago Press, 1960). For his latest position, see *Beyond Public Education* above, and Myron Lieberman, "Eggs That I Have Laid: Teacher Bargaining Reconsidered," *Phi Delta Kappan* 60, no. 6 (February, 1979): 415–19.

69. Magali Sarfatti Larson, *The Rise of Professionalism: A Sociological Analysis* (Berkeley: University of California Press, 1977), 9–18.

Chapter Five. The Modern Critique

1. Manfred Stanley, *The Technological Conscience: Survival and Dignity in the Age of Expertise* (Chicago: University of Chicago Press, 1978), 69–70.

2. See, for example, Gregory H. Davis, *Technology—Humanism and Nihilism* (Washington: University Press of America, 1981), 65–69; Erich

Fromm, *The Revolution of Hope* (New York: Bantan Books, 1968), 6–26; and Jacques Ellul, *The Technological Society* (New York: Vintage Books, 1964), 410–15.

3. Donald A. Schon, *The Reflective Practitioner: How Professionals Think in Action* (New York: Basic Books, 1983), 3–20.

4. Robert Nisbet, *History of the Idea of Progress* (New York: Basic Books, 1980), 347–49. Nisbet's argument is that the inflated pretentions of social science led to heightened cultural expectations that were unreachable. When the expectations were not fulfilled, rational knowledge itself was called into question.

5. Randall Collins, *The Credential Society* (New York: Academic Press, 1979), 135–38.

6. Schon, *The Reflective Practitioner,* 326–27.

7. Julien Freund, *The Sociology of Max Weber,* trans. May Ilford (New York: Vintage Books, 1969), 18.

8. This point is made by Richard Pratte, *The Public School Movement* (New York: David McKay Company, 1973), 102–104.

9. Schon, *The Reflective Practitioner,* 13–14.

10. Ibid., 30–37.

11. Quoted in Schon, *The Reflective Practitioner,* 24.

12. Bruce O. Watkins and Roy Meader, *Technology and Human Values* (Ann Arbor: Ann Arbor Science Publications, 1977), 125.

13. A. W. Combs, *Myths in Education: Beliefs that Hinder Progress and Their Alternatives* (Boston: Allyn and Bacon, 1979).

14. David Nyberg and Kieran Egan, *The Erosion of Education: Socialization and the Schools* (New York: Teachers College Press, 1981), 105–13.

15. Henry J. Perkinson, *The Imperfect Panacea: American Faith in Education, 1865–1990* (New York: McGraw-Hill, 1991).

16. The current debate over the effectiveness of sex and drug education curriculums center on the same concerns. Many advocates of the programs argue that teachers need to be better prepared, program objectives need better definition, and course work needs to be instituted throughout the curriculum. Detractors point out that a simple increase in knowledge and information will not change youthful attitudes. Drug abuse and teenage pregnancies rise because factors other than knowledge influence teenage behavior. Both sides generally agree that school programs alone will not work, and that other institutions will also need to get involved. For good discussions of this debate as

well as discussions of effectiveness research, see Michael S. Goodstadt, "School-based Drug Education in North America: What Is Wrong? What Can Be Done?," *Journal of School Health* 56, no. 7 (September, 1986): 278–81; and Douglas Kirby, "Sexuality Education: A More Realistic View of its Effects," *Journal of School Health* 55, no. 10 (December, 1985): 421–24.

17. Ellul, *Technological Society*, 79–147.

18. Nyberg and Egan, *The Erosion of Education*, 105–108.

19. Richard J. Murnane, "Understanding the Sources of Teaching Competence: Choices, Skills, and the Limits of Training," *Teachers College Record* 84, no. 3 (Spring, 1983): 564–69.

20. C. A. Bowers, "Rethinking Teacher Education: This Time Let's Get It Right," *Teachers College Record* 84, no. 3 (Spring, 1983): 557–63.

21. Joel Spring, *The American School 1642–1985* (New York: Longman, 1986), 319–23.

22. The Holmes Group, *Tomorrow's Teachers* (East Lansing, Mich.: The Holmes Group, 1986), 52.

23. Philip W. Jackson, *Life in Classrooms* (New York: Holt, Rinehart and Winston, 1968).

24. Ibid., vii.

25. Ibid., 4–11.

26. Ibid., 17.

27. Ibid., 18.

28. Ibid., 30.

29. Ibid., 11.

30. Ibid., 124–26.

31. Ibid., 126–43.

32. Ibid., 133.

33. Ibid., 143.

34. Ibid., 144–46.

35. Ibid., 149.

36. Ibid., 163–69.

37. Ibid., 149.

38. Ibid., 152.

39. Ibid., 153.

40. Philip W. Jackson, *The Practice of Teaching* (New York: Teachers College Press, 1986), 131.

41. Ibid., 137–41.

42. Ibid., 140.

43. Ibid., 125.

44. Ibid., 120–26.

45. Ibid., 144–45.

46. Alan Tom, *Teaching as a Moral Craft* (New York: Longman, 1984).

47. Ibid., 15–36.

48. Ibid., 55.

49. Ibid., 47.

50. Ibid., 43–45.

51. Ibid., 47–51.

52. Ibid., 66–68.

53. Ibid., 56.

54. Ibid., 63.

55. Ibid., 59–60.

56. Ibid., 71.

57. Ibid., 72.

58. Ibid.

59. Ibid., 128.

60. Ibid., 79–97.

61. Hannah Arendt, *Between Past and Future* (New York: Viking Press, 1961), 173–96.

62. Tom, *Teaching as a Moral Craft*, 142–43.

63. Ibid., 128.

64. Ibid., 121–25.

65. Ibid., 152–83.

66. Alan Tom, *How Should Teachers Be Educated? An Assessment of Three Reform Reports,* Fastback no. 255 (Bloomington, Ind.: Phi Delta Kappan Educational Foundation, 1987).

67. Tom, *Teaching as a Moral Craft,* 184–91.

68. Alan Tom, "Replacing Pedagogical Knowledge with Pedagogical Questions," in John Smyth, ed., *Educating Teachers: Changing the Nature of Pedagogical Knowledge* (London: The Falmer Press, 1987), 9.

69. Arendt, *Between Past and Future,* 27.

70. Yet Tom realizes that frequently preservice teachers want only advice about technical matters and survival techniques despite the best efforts of teacher educators. See Alan R. Tom, "The Practical Art of Redesigning Teacher Education: Teacher Education Reform at Washington University, 1970–1975," *Peabody Journal of Education* 65, no. 2 (Winter, 1988): 158–79.

71. Linda Vali and Alan Tom, "How Adequate Are the Knowledge Base Frameworks in Teacher Education?," *Journal of Teacher Education* 39, no. 5 (September/October, 1988): 5–12.

72. See Alan R. Tom, "The Holmes Group Report: Its Latent Political Agenda," *Teachers College Record* 88, no. 3 (Spring, 1987): 430–35; _____, A Semi-Professional Conception of Teaching," *Social Education* 51, no. 7 (November/December, 1987): 506–508; and Philip Jackson, "Facing Our Ignorance," *Teachers College Record* 88, no. 3 (Spring, 1987): 384–89.

73. Magali Sarfetti Larson, *The Rise of Professionalism: A Sociological Analysis* (Berkeley: University of California Press, 1977), xviii, 4–8.

74. Paul Goodman, "The New Reformation" in Irving Howe, ed., *Beyond the New Left* (New York: McCall, 1970), 86.

75. Schon, *The Reflective Practitioner,* 21–69.

76. Herbert Kohl, *On Teaching* (New York: Schocken Books, 1976).

Chapter Six. Expertise, Postmodernism, and Critical Pedagogy

1. Among other accounts, see Magali Sarfatti Larson, *The Rise of Professionalism: A Sociological Analysis* (Berkeley: University of California Press, 1977), 136–58.

2. The two books by Donald Schon have been the most widely regarded in making this point. See Donald A. Schon, *The Reflective Practitioner: How Professionals Think in Action* (New York: Basic Books, 1983), and *Educating the Reflective Practitioner* (San Francisco: Jossey-Bass Publishers, 1987).

3. Postmodernism is a term of great contention as thinkers and theorists in fields ranging through art, literature, architecture, film, dance, social science, philosophy, science, and social criticism have struggled to outline those aspects of the contemporary scene that separate it from the immediate past. Accordingly, the literature on postmodernism is vast, complex, and frequently insistent and strenuously assertive. For more general, readable discussions, see Charles Jencks and Maggie Keswick, *What Is Post-Modernism?* (New York: St. Martin's Press, 1987); Ihab Hassan, *The Postmodern Turn: Essays in Postmodern Theory and Culture* (Columbus: Ohio State University Press, 1987); A. Ross, ed., *Universal Abandon? The Politics of Postmodernism* (Minneapolis: University of Minneapolis Press, 1988); Matei Calinescu, *Five Faces of Modernity: Modernism, Avant-Garde, Decadence, Kitsch, Postmodernism* (Durham, N.C.: Duke University Press, 1987); Jonathon Arac, ed., *Postmodernism and Politics* (Minneapolis: University of Minnesota Press, 1986); and Todd Gitlin, "Postmodernism: Roots and Politics," *Dissent* 36 (Winter, 1989): 100–108.

4. Jean-Francois Lyotard, *The Postmodern Condition: A Report on Knowledge* (Minneapolis: University of Minnesota Press, 1979), 4–5.

5. Larson, *The Rise of Professionalism*, 40–53.

6. Lyotard, *The Postmodern Condition*, 8–23. See also Richard Rorty, *Contingency, Irony, and Solidarity* (Cambridge: Cambridge University Press, 1989), 3–22; and Paul Feyerabend, *Against Method: Outline of an Anarchistic Theory of Knowledge* (London: Western Printing Services, 1975).

7. Jean Baudrillard, *Selected Writings*, M. Poster, ed., (Stanford: Stanford University Press, 1988), 166–84. See also Neil Postman, *Amusing Ourselves to Death* (New York: Viking, 1985).

8. Lyotard, *The Postmodern Condition*, 60–67.

9. I am indebted to Henry Giroux for this description. See Henry A. Giroux, "Postmodernism and the Discourse of Educational Criticism," *Journal of Education* 170, no. 3 (1988): 5–30.

10. Ironically Lyotard posits, in distinction from Rorty, that the postmodern poet strives to be more like a philosopher. This seeming contradiction, however, actually flows from the same source — the understanding that the postmodern thinker cannot rest on any surity or understanding of a higher truth. Thus Lyotard writes, "A postmodern artist or writer is in the position of the philosopher: the text he writes, the work he produces are not in principle governed by preestablished rules, and they cannot be judged according to a predetermining judgement, by applying familiar categories to the text or to the work. Those rules and categories are what the work of art itself is looking for. The artist and the writer, then, are working without rules in order to formulate the rules of what *will later have been done.* Hence the fact that the work and text have the character of an *event.*" Lyotard, *The Postmodern Condition*, 84.

11. Richard Rorty, *Philosophy and the Mirror of Nature* (Princeton: Princeton University Press, 1979).

12. Rorty argues that the poet as opposed to the philosopher understands that the philosophical project of discovering a permanent, ahistorical, context for human life should be given up for the embrace of discontinuity. Rorty notes the modern "tension between an effort to achieve universality by the recognition of contingency and the effort to achieve universality by the transcendence of contingency." In his view, "the important philosophers of our own century are those who have tried to follow through on the Romantic poets by breaking with Plato and seeing freedom as the recognition of contingency. They are the philosophers who have...tried to avoid anything that smacks of philosophy as contemplation, as the attempt to see life steadily and see it whole, in order to insist on contingency of individual existence." Rorty, *Contingency, Irony, and Solidarity*, 23–26.

13. The literature offering a feminist perspective on pedagogy is wide and growing. See Carol Gilligan, *In a Different Voice* (Cambridge: Harvard University Press, 1982); Nel Noddings, *Caring: A Feminine Approach to Ethics and Moral Education* (Berkeley: University of California Press, 1982); Madeline Grumet, *Bitter Milk: Women and Teaching* (Amherst: University of Mass. Press, 1988); Landon Beyer, Walter Feinberg, Jo Anne Pagano, and James Anthony Whitson, *Preparing Teachers as Professionals: The Role of Educational Studies and Other Liberal Disciplines* (New York: Teachers College Press, 1989), 97–116; and Susan Laird, "Reforming 'Women's True Profession': A Case for 'Feminist Pedagogy' in Teacher Education?," *Harvard Educational Review* 58, no. 4 (November, 1988): 449–63.

14. Lawrence Kohlberg, *The Philosophy of Moral Development* (New York: Harper and Row, 1981).

15. Gilligan, *In a Different Voice*, 159–74.

16. Allan Bloom, *The Closing of the American Mind* (New York: Simon and Schuster, 1987); E. D. Hirsch, *Cultural Literacy: What Every American Needs to Know* (Boston: Houghton Mifflin, 1987); Diane Ravitch and Chester E. Finn, Jr., *What Do Our 17-Year-Olds Know?* (New York: Harper and Row, 1987); and Mortimer Adler, *The Paideia Proposal* (New York: Macmillan, 1982).

17. Bloom, *The Closing of the American Mind*, 379.

18. Daniel Bell, *The Cultural Contradictions of Capitalism* (New York: Basic Books, 1976), 51–55.

19. For the conservative position, see Thomas Sowell, *Education: Assumptions vs. History* (Stanford: Hoover Press, 1986); Diane Ravitch and Chester E. Finn, Jr., eds., *Against Mediocrity* (New York: Holmes and Meier, 1984); Diane Ravitch, *The Schools We Deserve*, (New York: Basic Books, 1985); and Edward

Winne, "The Great Tradition in Education: Transmitting Moral Values," *Educational Leadership* 43, no. 4 (December, 1985): 4–9.

20. Robert N. Bellah, et al., *Habits of the Heart* (New York: Harper and Row, 1985); Christopher Lasch, *The Culture of Narcissism* (New York: Warner Books, 1979); and *The Minimal Self: Psychic Survival in Troubled Times* (New York: W. W. Norton, 1984).

21. Lasch, *The Culture of Narcissism*, 228–32.

22. Foremost among these may be Henry Giroux and Maxine Greene, whose thought is critiqued below. But also see C. A. Bowers, *Elements of a Post-Liberal Theory of Education* (New York: Teachers College Press, 1987); Thomas S. Popkewitz, ed., *Critical Studies in Education* (London: The Falmer Press, 1987); Harvey Holtz, et al., *Education and the American Dream* (Granby, Mass.: Bergin and Garvey, 1989); and Paulo Friere, *The Politics of Education: Culture Power and Liberation* (Hadley, Mass.: Bergin and Garvey, 1985).

23. Thomas L. Haskell, *The Emergence of Professional Social Science: The American Social Science Association and the Nineteenth-Century Crisis of Authority* (Urbana, Ill.: University of Illinois Press, 1977), 67.

24. As Greene writes, "There will be no closure for us; there cannot be. The questions...remain open: the questions having to do with defining education, determining educational purposes, achieving democracy." Maxine Greene, *The Teacher as Stranger* (Belmont, California: Wadsworth Publishing Company, 1973), 270–71.

25. Maxine Greene, *The Public School and the Private Vision* (New York: Random House, 1965).

26. Ibid., 6.

27. Greene, *The Teacher as Stranger*, 8.

28. Ibid., 6–7.

29. Ibid., 8.

30. Ibid., 9.

31. Ibid., 20.

32. Maxine Greene, "How Do We Think About Our Craft?," *Teachers College Record* 86, no. 1 (Fall, 1984): 55.

33. Maxine Greene, *Dialectic of Freedom* (New York: Teachers College Press, 1988), 4.

34. Ibid., 9.

35. Ibid., 16.

36. Greene, *The Teacher as Stranger,* 21.

37. Greene, "How Do We Think About Our Craft?," 58–59.

38. Greene, *The Teacher as Stranger,* preface.

39. Ibid., 267–98.

40. Ibid., 274–75.

41. Ibid., 272.

42. Greene, "How Do We Think About Our Craft?," 61.

43. Ibid., 60.

44. Maxine Greene, "Teaching: The Question of Personal Reality," *Teachers College Record* 80, no. 1 (September, 1978): 23–35.

45. Greene, "How Do We Think About Our Craft?," 57.

46. Ibid., 63.

47. Ibid., 66.

48. This seems true even as Greene turns to focus directly on the need for a critical pedagogy in the United States. Her purpose in such an exposition does include comment about the exclusion of different voices from the educational experience, but the body of her writing dwells less on this than tracing in literature and history how people have challenged the prevailing order. In this way, the public dimension is affected, but always with the overriding concern for individual liberation. Thus she argues, "We cannot negate the fact of power. But we can undertake a resistance, a reaching out towards becoming *persons* among other persons, for all the talk of human resources, for all the orienting of education to the economy. To engage with our students as persons is to affirm our own incompleteness, our consciousness of spaces still to be explored, desires still to be tapped, possibilities still to be opened and pursued." Maxine Greene, "In Search of a Critical Pedagogy," *Teachers College Record* 56, no. 4 (November, 1986): 440.

49. Paulo Friere, *Pedagogy of the Oppressed* (New York: Herder and Herder, 1971). This remains Friere's most influential work. For other works, see Paulo Friere, *Education for Critical Consciousness* (New York: Seabury Press, 1973); ———, *Pedagogy in Process: The Letters to Guinea-Bissau* (New York: Seabury Press, 1978); and ———, *The Politics of Education: Culture, Power and Liberation* (Hadley, Mass.: Bergin and Garvey, 1985).

50. It is impossible to cite all the important sources of this literature. A substantial amount of it flows from Giroux. For recent expositions, see Peter

McClaren, *Life in Schools* (New York: Longman, 1989); David I. Purpel, *The Moral and Spiritual Crisis in Education* (New York: Bergin and Garvey, 1989); Thomas S. Popkewitz, ed., *Critical Studies in Teacher Education* (London: Falmer Press, 1987); Henry A. Giroux and Peter McClaren, eds., *Critical Pedagogy, the State and Cultural Struggle* (Albany: State University of New York Press, 1989); and Daniel P. Liston and Kenneth M. Zeichner, "Critical Pedagogy and Teacher Education," *Journal of Education* 169 (1987): 117–37.

51. See Michael Katz, *The Irony of Early School Reform: Educational Innovation in Mid-Nineteenth Century Massachusetts* (Cambridge: Harvard University Press, 1968); M. F. D. Young, ed., *Knowledge and Control* (London: Collier-Macmillan, 1971); Basil Bernstein, *Class, Codes and Control*, Vol. 3 (London: Routledge and Kegan Paul, 1977); Michael Apple, *Ideology and Curriculum* (London: Routledge and Kegan Paul, 1977); and Clarence J. Karier, Paul C. Violas, and Joel Spring, *Roots of Crisis: American Education in the Twentieth Century* (Chicago: Rand McNally, 1973).

52. The classic sources for this idea are Samuel Bowles and Herbert Gintis, *Schooling In Capitalist America* (New York: Basic Books, 1976); and Paul Willis, *Learning to Labor: How Working Class Kids Get Working Class Jobs* (New York: Columbia University Press, 1981).

53. One of the major challenges of postmodern thought, of course, is directed against any attempt to narrow meaning within any one cultural discourse. Similarly, one of the areas that has been of the most interest to critical pedagogy has been the area of literacy. Literacy refers to far more than technical skill in this view, it refers to the capacity to develop and interpret the world. See Peter McClaren, "Culture or Canon? Critical Pedagogy and the Politics of Literacy," *Harvard Educational Review* 58 no. 2 (May, 1988): 213–34.

54. Henry A. Giroux, "Rethinking Education Reform in the Age of George Bush," *Phi Delta Kappan* 70, no. 9 (May, 1989): 728–30.

55. Giroux sees this as a limitation of his earlier work. See Henry A. Giroux, *Teachers as Intellectuals* (Granby, Mass.: Bergin and Garvey, 1988), xxiv.

56. Henry A. Giroux, *Ideology, Culture, and the Process of Schooling* (Philadelphia: Temple University Press, 1981), 98–101.

57. Stanley Aronowitz and Henry A. Giroux, *Education Under Siege* (South Hadley, Mass.: Bergin and Garvey, 1985), 79.

58. Giroux, *Ideology, Culture, and the Process of Schooling*, 50–53.

59. Henry A. Giroux, "Teachers as Transformative Intellectuals," *Social Education* 58 (May, 1985): 376–79.

60. Giroux, *Teachers as Intellectuals*, 73.

61. Aronowitz and Giroux, *Education Under Siege*, 28.

62. Giroux, *Ideology, Culture, and the Process of Schooling*, 53.

63. Henry A. Giroux, *Schooling and the Struggle for Public Life* (Minneapolis: University of Minnesota Press, 1988), 121.

64. Stanley Aronowitz and Henry A. Giroux, "Schooling, Culture, and Literacy in the Age of Broken Dreams: A Review of Hirsch and Bloom," *Harvard Educational Review* 58, no. 2 (May, 1988): 194.

65. Ibid., 194.

66. Giroux, *Schooling and the Struggle for Public Life*, 103.

67. Aronowitz and Giroux, *Education Under Siege*, 156.

68. Ibid., 157.

69. Ibid., 158–59.

70. Ibid., 23–43.

71. Ibid., 33.

72. Ibid., 34.

73. Giroux, *Schooling and the Struggle for Public Life*, 109.

74. Aronowitz and Giroux, *Education Under Siege*, 34–40.

75. Giroux, *Schooling and the Struggle for Public Life*, xii.

76. Ibid., 37.

77. Ibid., 90.

78. Elizabeth Ellsworth recently criticized those in the critical pedagogy movement for adopting simple-minded conceptions of dialogue and voice, as if the separate lives of different students are easily bridged. Thus, she notes, "Dialogue in its conventional sense is impossible in the culture at large because at this historical moment, power relations between race, classed, and gendered students and teachers are unjust. The injustice of these relations and the way in which those injustices distort communication cannot be overcome in a classroom, no matter how committed the teacher and students are to 'overcoming conditions that perpetuate suffering.'" Elizabeth Ellsworth, "Why Doesn't This Feel Empowering? Working Through the Repressive Myths of Critical Pedagogy," *Harvard Educational Review* 59, no. 3 (August, 1989): 316. Giroux saw this view as denying the possibilities of collective action and as being "less an insight than a crippling form of political disengagement." Henry A. Giroux, "Border Pedagogy in the Age of Postmodernism," *Journal of Education* 170, no. 3 (1988): 177–78.

79. Giroux, *Schooling and the Struggle for Public Life*, 102–103.

80. Greene, *Dialectic of Freedom*, 12.

81. Ibid., 9.

82. Giroux, "Border Pedagogy in the Age of Postmodernism," 178.

83. Giroux, *Schooling and the Struggle for Public Life*, 68.

84. Bowers, *Elements of a Post-Liberal Theory of Education*, 151.

85. Giroux, *Schooling and the Struggle for Public Life*, 68.

86. Bowers, *Elements of a Post-Liberal Theory of Education*, 125.

87. Hannah Arendt, *Between Past and Future* (New York: Viking Press, 1961), 192–93.

88. Ibid., 195.

Chapter Seven. Conclusion

1. Edith Hamilton and Huntington Cairns, eds., *The Collected Dialogues of Plato* (Princeton, N.J.: Princeton University Press, 1969), 308–52.

2. This scholarship originates in psychological studies that attempt to explain the way experts process information and form judgments in fields as separate as chess and physics. For examples of research attempts to analyze the differences between how master and beginning teachers handle instructional problems, see Lee S. Schulman, "Knowledge and Teaching," *Harvard Educational Review* 57, no. 1 (February, 1987): 1–22; K. Carter, K. Cushing, D. Sabers, P. Stein, and D. Berliner, "Expert–Novice Differences in Perceiving and Processing Visual Classroom Stimuli," *Journal of Teacher Education* 39, no. 3 (1988): 25–31; A. M. Lesgold, "Acquiring Expertise," in J. R. Anderson and S. M Kosslyn, eds., *Tutorials in Learning and Memory* (San Francisco: W. H. Freeman, 1984), 31–60; and Carol Livingston and Hilda Borko, "Expert–Novice Differences in Teaching: A Cognitive Analysis and Implications for Teacher Education," *Journal of Teacher Education* 40, no. 4, (1989): 36–42.

3. David C. Berliner, "The Development of Expertise in Pedagogy," Charles W. Hunt Memorial Lecture presented at the annual meeting of the American Association of Colleges of Teacher Education, New Orleans, La. (February, 1988).

4. In addition to the above, see David C. Berliner, "In Pursuit of the Expert Pedagogue," *Educational Researcher* 15 (August/September, 1986): 5–13.

5. For an excellent account of how this affects the perception of teachers,

see Sigrun Gudmundsdottir, "Values in Pedagogical Content Knowledge," *Journal of Teacher Education* 41, no. 3 (1990): 44–52; Nancy W. Brickhouse, "Teachers' Beliefs About the Nature of Science and Their Relationship to Classroom Practice," *Journal of Teacher Education* 41, no. 4 (1990): 53–62; and Nona Lyons, "Dilemmas of Knowing: Ethical and Epistemological Dimensions of Teachers' Work and Development," *Harvard Educational Review* 60, no. 2 (1990): 159–79.

6. An interesting aspect of the current research into expertise and teaching is that it follows a stage theory substantially articulated by philosophers. The point is to uncover those senses of intellect that distinguish human understanding from that of computers. See H. L. Dreyfus and S. E. Dreyfus, *Mind Over Machine* (New York: Free Press, 1986).

7. See, for example, Garret Keizer, *No Place but Here: A Teacher's Vocation in a Rural Community* (New York: Viking, 1988); Eliot Wigginton, *Sometimes a Shining Moment: The Foxfire Experience* (New York: Anchor Press/Doubleday, 1985); and Carol Stumbo, "Beyond the Classroom," *Harvard Educational Review* 59, no. 1 (1989): 87–97. For accounts of teachers, see Mary E. Bredemeier, *Urban Classroom Portraits: Teachers Who Make a Difference* (New York: P. Lang Publishers, 1988), and Tracy Kidder, *Among Schoolchildren* (Boston: Houghton Mifflin, 1989).

8. Jessica Howard, "On Teaching, Knowledge, and 'Middle Ground,'" *Harvard Educational Review* 59, no. 2 (1989): 226–39.

9. Ibid., 227.

10. John I. Goodlad, Roger Soder, Kenneth A. Sirotnik, eds., *The Moral Dimensions of Teaching* (San Francisco: Jossey-Bass Publishers, 1990).

11. See Nancy Hoffman, *Woman's "True" Profession: Voices from the History of Teaching* (Old Westbury, N.Y.: Feminist Press, 1981); Nel Noddings, *Caring: A Feminine Approach to Ethics and Moral Education* (Berkeley: University of California Press, 1984); Margo Culley and Catherine Portuges, eds., *Gendered Subjects: The Dynamics of Feminist Teaching* (Boston: Routledge and Kegan Paul, 1985); Madeline Grumet, *Bitter Milk: Women and Teaching* (Amherst: University of Massachusetts Press, 1988); and Susan Laird, "Reforming 'Woman's True Profession': A Case for 'Feminist Pedagogy' in Teacher Education?," *Harvard Educational Review* 58, no. 4 (1988): 449–63.

12. Jane Roland Martin, "Reforming Teacher Education, Rethinking Liberal Education," *Teachers College Record* 88, no. 3 (1987): 406–09.

13. Carolyn M. Shrewsbury, "What Is Feminist Pedagogy?," *Women's Studies Quarterly* 15 (Fall/Winter, 1987): 6.

14. Mary Field Belenky, Blythe McVicker Clinchy, Nancy Rule Goldberger, and Jill Mattuck Tarule, *Women's Ways of Knowing: The Development of Self, Voice, and Mind* (New York: Basic Books, 1986).

15. For a good discussion of the different implications of the new research on teaching, see Hugh T. Sockett, "Has Shulman Got the Strategy Right?," *Harvard Educational Review* 57, no. 2 (May, 1987): 208–19.

16. In a recent review of the literature, John L. Knapp and his colleagues found no evidence to warrant requiring a master's degree of all teachers. In an opposing response, Richard Turner also found little correlation between a master's degree and student achievement, though he argued that social expectations will force the requirement regardless. See John L. Knapp, Robert F. McNergney, Joanne M. Herbert, and Harold L. York, "Should a Master's Degree Be Required of All Teachers?," *Journal of Teacher Education* 41, no. 2 (1990): 27–37, and Richard Turner, "An Issue for the 1990's: The Efficacy of the Required Master's Degree," *Journal of Teacher Education* 41, no. 2 (1990): 38-44.

17. See Joseph S. Johnston, Jr., et al., *Those Who Can* (Washington, D.C.: Association of American Colleges, 1989), and Eva Foldes Travers and Susan Riemer Sacks, "Teacher Education and the Liberal Arts," *Education Digest* 53 (December, 1987): 9–11. For a more critical perspective, see Langdon Beyer, Walter Feinberg, JoAnn Pagano, and James Anthony Whitson, *Preparing Teachers as Professionals: The Role of Educational Studies and Other Descriptions* (New York: Teachers College Press, 1989).

18. This was a major theme of Giroux's recent work. See Henry A. Giroux, *Schooling and the Struggle for Public Life: Critical Pedagogy in the Modern Age* (Minneapolis: University of Minnesota Press, 1988). For other accounts, see Alasdair MacIntyre, *After Virtue* (Notre Dame, Ind.: University of Notre Dame Press, 1981), 1–22; Robert N. Bellah, et al., *Habits of the Heart* (Berkeley: University of California Press, 1985); and Christopher Lasch, *The Minimal Self: Psychic Survival in Troubled Times* (New York: W. W. Norton, 1984).

Selected Bibliography

Akin, William E. *Technocracy and the American Dream*. Berkeley: University of California Press, 1977.

Arendt, Hannah. *Between Past and Future*. New York: Penguin Books, 1968.

Aronowitz, Stanley, and Giroux, Henry A. *Education Under Siege*. South Hadley, Mass.: Bergin and Garvey, 1985.

Belenky, Mary Field; Clinchy, Blythe McVicker; and Goldberger, Nancy Rule. *Women's Ways of Knowing: The Development of Self, Voice, and Mind*. New York: Basic Books, 1986.

Bell, Daniel. *The Coming of Post-Industrial Society*. New York: Basic Books, 1973.

Berliner, David A. "The Development of Expertise in Pedagogy." Charles W. Hunt Memorial Lecture, American Association of Colleges of Teacher Education, New Orleans, La. (February, 1988).

Bernier, Norman R., and Williams, Jack E. *Beyond Beliefs: Ideological Foundations of American Education*. Englewood Cliffs, N.J.: Prentice-Hall, 1973.

Bledstein, Burton J. *The Culture of Professionalism*. New York: W.W. Norton, 1976.

Bloom, Alan. *The Closing of the American Mind*. New York: Simon and Schuster, 1987.

Borrowman, Merle J. *Teacher Education in America*. New York: Teachers College Press, 1965.

Bowers, C. A. *Elements of a Post-Liberal Theory of Education*. New York: Teachers College Press, 1987.

Bowers, C. A. *The Progressive Educator and the Depression*. New York: Random House, 1969.

170   SELECTED BIBLIOGRAPHY

Boyer, Ernest L. *High School: A Report on Secondary Education in America.* New York: Harper and Row, 1983.

Bruce-Briggs, B., ed. *The New Class?* New Brunswick, N.J.: Transaction Books, 1979.

Callahan, Raymond E. *Education and the Cult of Efficiency.* Chicago: University of Chicago Press, 1962.

Caplow, Theodore. *The Sociology of Work.* New York: McGraw Hill, 1954.

Carlton, Wendy. *"In Our Professional Opinion...": The Primacy of Clinical Judgement Over Professional Skills.* Notre Dame, Ind.: University of Notre Dame Press, 1978.

The Carnegie Forum of Education and the Economy, *A Nation Prepared: Teachers for the 21st Century.* New York: Carnegie Corporation, 1986.

Collins, Randall. *The Credential Society.* New York: Academic Press, 1979.

Counts, George S. *Dare the School Build a New Social Order?* New York: John Day Company, 1932.

Counts, George S. *The Social Composition of Boards of Education.* Chicago: University of Chicago Press, 1927.

Counts, George S. *The Social Foundations of Education.* New York: Charles Scribner's Sons, 1934.

Cremin, Lawerence. *The Genius of American Education.* New York: Vintage Books, 1965.

Cremin, Lawerence. *The Transformation of the School.* New York: Alfred A. Knopf, 1961.

Cremin, Lawerence. *The Wonderful World of Ellwood Patterson Cubberley.* New York: Bureau of Publications, Teachers College, Columbia University, 1965.

Cubberley, Ellwood P. *Changing Conceptions of Education.* Boston: Houghton Mifflin Company, 1922.

Cubberley, Ellwood P. *Public School Administration.* Boston: Houghton Mifflin Company, 1929.

Dennis, Lawrence J. *George S. Counts and Charles Beard: Collaborators for Change.* Albany: State University of New York Press, 1989.

Dennis, Lawrence J., and Eaton, William Edward. *George S. Counts: Educator for a New Age.* Carbondale: Southern Illinois University Press, 1980.

Dewey, John. *Sources of a Science of Education.* New York: Horace Liveright, 1929.

Elias, John L. *Conscientization and Deschooling*. Philadelphia: The Westminster Press, 1976.

Ellul, Jacques. *The Technological Society*. New York: Vintage Books, 1964.

Elsbree, Willard S. *The American Teacher*. New York: American Book Company, 1939.

Etzioni, Amitai, ed. *The Semi-Professions and Their Organizations*. New York: Free Press, 1969.

Featherstone, Joseph. *What Schools Can Do*. New York: Horace Liveright, 1976.

Flexner, Abraham. *Medical Education in the United States and Canada*. Carnegie Foundation Bulletin no. 4, New York: Carnegie Foundation, 1910.

Freidson, Eliot. *Profession of Medicine*. New York: Dodd, Mead and Company, 1970.

Friedenberg, Edgar. *Coming of Age in America*. New York: Random House, 1965.

Friedenberg, Edgar. *The Vanishing Adolescent*. New York: Dell Publishing, 1959.

Friere, Paulo. *Pedagogy of the Oppressed*. New York: Herder and Herder, 1971.

Friere, Paulo. *The Politics of Education*. Hadley, Mass.: Bergin and Garvey, 1985.

Galbraith, John Kenneth. *The New Industrial State*. New York: Signet Books, 1968.

Gartner, Alan; Greer, Colin; and Riessman, Frank, eds. *After Deschooling, What?*. New York: Harper and Row, 1973.

Gilligan, Carol. *In a Different Voice*. Cambridge: Harvard University Press, 1982.

Giroux, Henry A. "Border Pedagogy in the Age of Postmodernism." *Journal of Education* 170, no. 3 (1988): 162–81.

Giroux, Henry A. *Ideology, Culture, and the Process of Schooling*. Philadelphia: Temple University Press, 1981.

Giroux, Henry A. *Schooling and the Struggle for Public Life*. Minneapolis: University of Minnesota Press, 1988.

Goode, William J.; Furstenberg, Frank F.; and Mitchell, Larry R., eds. *Willard Waller: On the Family, Education, and War*. Chicago: University of Chicago Press, 1970.

Goodlad, John I. *A Place Called School*. New York: McGraw-Hill, 1984.

Goodlad, John I.; Soder, Roger; and Sirotnik, Kenneth A., eds. *The Moral Dimensions of Teaching*. San Francisco: Jossey-Bass, 1990.

Goodman, Paul. *Compulsory Mis-education and the Community of Scholars*. New York: Vintage Books, 1964.

Goodman, Paul. *Growing Up Absurd*. New York: Vintage Books, 1960.

Gould, Stephen Jay. *The Mismeasure of Man*. New York: W.W. Norton, 1981.

Greene, Maxine. *Dialectic of Freedom*. New York: Teachers College Press, 1988.

Greene, Maxine. "How We Think About Our Craft?" *Teachers College Record* 86, no. 1 (Fall, 1984): 55–67.

Greene, Maxine. *The Teacher as Stranger*. Belmont, Calif.: Wadsworth Publishing, 1973.

Gutek, Gerald L. *The Educational Theory of George S. Counts*. Columbus, Ohio: Ohio State University Press, 1970.

Haber, Samuel. *Efficiency and Uplift*. Chicago: University of Chicago Press, 1964.

Haskell, Thomas L., ed. *The Authority of Experts*. Bloomington, Ind.: Indiana University Press, 1984.

Hirsch, E. D. *Cultural Literacy: What Every American Needs to Know*. Boston: Houghton Mifflin, 1987.

Hofstadter, Richard. *Anti-intellectualism in American Life*. New York: Alfred A. Knopf, 1964.

The Holmes Group. *Tomorrow's Teachers*. East Lansing, Mich.: The Holmes Group, 1986.

Holt, John. *How Children Fail*. New York: Delacorte Press, 1982.

Illich, Ivan. *Celebration of Awareness*. Garden City, N.Y.: Doubleday and Company, 1970.

Illich, Ivan. *Deschooling Society*. New York: Harper and Row, 1971.

Illich, Ivan. *Medical Nemesis*. New York: Pantheon Books, 1976.

Illich, Ivan, et al. *Disabling Professions*. Boston: Marion Boyars, 1979.

Jackson, Philip W. "Facing Our Ignorance." *Teachers College Record* 88, no. 3 (1987): 384–89.

Jackson, Philip W. *Life in Classrooms*. New York: Holt, Rinehart, and Winston, 1968.

Jackson, Philip W. *The Practice of Teaching.* New York: Teachers College Press, 1986.

James, William. *Talks to Teachers on Psychology and to Students on Some of Life's Ideals.* New York: Henry Holt and Company, 1916.

Johnson, Terence J. *Professions and Power.* London: Macmillan Press, 1972.

Kohl, Herbert. *On Teaching.* New York: Schocken Books, 1976.

Kohl, Herbert. *36 Children.* New York: New American Library, 1967.

Kozol, Jonathan. *Death at an Early Age.* Boston: Houghton Mifflin, 1967.

Kozol, Jonathan. *The Night Is Dark and I Am Far from Home.* Boston: Houghton Mifflin, 1975.

Lagemann, Ellen Condliffe, ed. *Jane Addams on Education.* New York: Teachers College Press, 1985.

Lapp, Ralph E. *The New Priesthood: The Scientific Elite and the Uses of Power.* New York: Harper and Row, 1965.

Larson, Magali Sarfetti. *The Rise of Professionalism: A Sociological Analysis.* Berkeley: University of California Press, 1977.

Lasch, Christopher. *The Culture of Narcissism.* New York: Warner Books, 1979.

Lasch, Christopher. *The Minimal Self: Psychic Survival in Troubled Times.* New York: W.W. Norton, 1984.

Lewis, C. S. *The Abolition of Man.* London: Oxford University Press, 1944.

Lieberman, Myron. *Beyond Public Education.* New York: Praeger Publishers, 1986.

Lortie, Daniel C. "Laymen to Lawmen: Law School, Careers, and Socialization." *Harvard Educational Review* 29, no. 4 (1959): 352–59.

Lortie, Daniel C. *Schoolteacher: A Sociological Study.* Chicago: University of Chicago Press, 1975.

Lortie, Daniel C. "The Teacher's Shame: Anger and the Normative Commitments of Classrooom Teachers." *School Review* 75, no. 2 (1967): 155–71.

Lyotard, Jean-Francois. *The Postmodern Condition: A Report on the Condition of Knowledge.* Minneapolis: University of Minnesota Press, 1979.

MacIntrye, Alasdair. *After Virtue.* Notre Dame, Ind.: University of Notre Dame Press, 1981.

McLaren, Peter. *Life in Schools.* New York: Longman, 1989.

Nisbet, Robert. *History of the Idea of Progress*. New York: Basic Books, 1980.

Noddings, Nel. *Caring: A Feminine Approach to Ethics and Moral Education*. Berkeley: University of California Press, 1982.

Nyberg, David, and Egan, Kieran. *The Erosion of Education: Socialization and the Schools*. New York: Teachers College Press, 1981.

Perkinson, Henry J. *The Imperfect Panacea: American Faith in the Schools, 1865–1990*. New York: McGraw-Hill, 1991.

Perkinson, Henry J. *Two Hundred Years of American Educational Thought*. New York: David McKay Company, 1976.

Pirsig, Robert. *Zen and the Art of Motorcycle Maintenance*. New York: Bantam Books, 1974.

Ravitch, Diane. *The Schools We Deserve*. New York: Basic Books, 1985.

Rorty, Richard. *Contingency, Irony, and Solidarity*. Cambridge: Cambridge University Press, 1989.

Ross, A., ed. *Universal Abandon? The Politics of Postmodernism*. Minneapolis: University of Minnesota Press, 1988.

Roszak, Theodore. *Making of a Counter Culture*. New York: Doubleday and Company, 1968.

Schon, Donald A. *Educating the Reflective Practitioner*. San Francisco: Jossey-Bass, 1987.

Schon, Donald A. *The Reflective Practitioner: How Professionals Think in Action*. New York: Basic Books, 1983.

Sears, Jesse B., and Henderson, Adin D. *Cubberley of Stanford*. Stanford: Stanford University Press, 1957.

Seeley, David S. *Education Through Partnership*. Washington, D.C.: American Enterprise Institute for Public Policy Research, 1985.

Segal, Howard P. *Technological Utopianism in American Culture*. Chicago: University of Chicago Press, 1985.

Sizer, Theodore. *Horace's Compromise: The Dilemma of the American High School*. Boston: Houghton Mifflin, 1984.

Smyth, John, ed. *Educating Teachers: Changing the Nature of Pedagogical Knowledge*. London: The Falmer Press, 1987.

Spring, Joel. *American Education: An Introduction to Social and Political Aspects*. New York: Longman, 1991.

Spring, Joel. *The American School 1642–1985.* New York: Longman, 1986.

Stanley, Manfred. *The Technological Conscience: Survival and Dignity in the Age of Expertise.* Chicago: University of Chicago Press, 1978.

Tom, Alan R. "The Holmes Group Report: Its Latent Political Agenda." *Teachers College Record* 88, no. 3 (1987): 430–35.

Tom, Alan R. *Teaching as a Moral Craft.* New York: Longman, 1984.

Tyack, David B. *The One Best System.* Cambridge: Harvard University Press, 1974.

Tyack, David, and Hansot, Elisabeth. *Managers of Virtue: Public School Leadership in America, 1820–1980.* New York: Basic Books, 1982.

Waller, Willard. *The Sociology of Teaching.* New York: John Wiley and Sons, 1932.

Wilensky, Harold L. "The Professionalization of Everyone?" *The American Journal of Sociology* 70, no. 2 (1964): 137–58.

Index

Epimetheus, 77, 98

Ethos of teaching, 58–60

Etzioni, Amitai, 54, 57

Expertise; development of, 2–3; and
dignity, 83–84; in educational
administration, 20–21; and educational reform, 8–11; and educational specialization, 6–8; faith in,
17; feminist critique of, 103–104
moral limits of, 4–6; postmodern
critique of, 101–103; and profes-
sional/client relations, 5–6, 34–37;
and professionalism in education,
42–44, 45–48, 61–64; psychological understanding of, 130–131,
165; and technological/bureau-
cratic obscurity, 3–4, 83–84; and
technological growth, 15–17. *See
also* Knowledge; Professionalization; Specialization; Technocracy;
and the names of specific theorists

Featherstone, Joseph, review of Lortie, 62–63

Feminism: critique of expertise,
103–104; critique of professionalization, 38; of teaching, 132–133

Flexner, Alexander, 47

Fischer, Frank, 5

Freedom: Greene's conception of,
109; negative view, 81; and
romanticism, 78, 80–81

Free school movement, 78

Freidson, Eliot, 34

Freud, Sigmund, 109

Friedenberg, Edgar Z., 65, 70–71,
75, 77; compared to Goodman, 70;
and social conflict, 70

Friedman, Milton, 81, 129

Friere, Paulo, 119, politics of literacy,
114

Galbraith, John Kenneth, 2

Gilligan, Carol, 103, 104

Giroux, Henry, 12–13, 115–122,
125–128, 130, 131, 133, 134; analysis of knowledge, 117–118; compared with Greene, 123–125; concept of voice, 118–120; criticism
of, 126–128; critique of
Bloom/Hirsch, 118; critique of
correspondence theory, 116–117;
intellectual background, 115–117;
on public responsibility, 121–122;
on teachers as transformative
intellectuals, 120–121, 125, 135

Goode, William J., 56, 57

Goodlad, John, 56, 132

Goodman, Paul, 4, 65, 68–71, 75, 77,
77, 99; compared to Friedenberg,
70; critical orientation, 68, 70; critique of programmed instruction,
69–70

Greene, Maxine, 12, 13, 105–113,
123–128, 131, 133; compared with
Giroux, 123–125; and critical pedagogy, 113–114, 162; critique of
Bloom/Hirsch, 112; on freedom
and intellectual responsibility,
108–109, 111, 113; intellectual
background, 106–108; on moral
and public responsibility,
110–111, 124

Grumet, Madeline, 103

Haber, Samuel, 18

Hall, G. Stanley, 17

Haskell, Thomas, 3, 105

Herbart, Johann Friedrich, 42

Hidden curriculum, 76, 89, 114–115

Hirsch, E. D., criticized by
Greene/Giroux, 112, 118, 119

Hofstadter, Richard, 45, 67

Holmes, Henry W., 9, 32

Holmes Report (*Tomorrow's Teachers:
A Report of the Holmes Group*), 99,
132; support of expertise, 9–10;
and technical rationality, 87

Holt, John, 65, 73–75, 77, 78, 100;

Teacher effectiveness research: Tom's critique of, 92–95

Teachers/teaching: and accountability, 55–56; affected by classroom climate, 50, 53–54, 58, 88–90; ethos of, 57–60; as feminine vocation, 16, 46–47, 103–104, 132–133; five year degree, 167; knowledge base of, 42–43, 46, 59–60, 85–87, 104, 131–133; language of, 135; metaphors of, 17, 95, 142; progressive understanding of, 17–18, 24–25; qualities of, 89–90, 97–98; and science, 4, 25–26, 87, 96, 136; search for professional status, 42–44, 45, 48, 61–64; social reconstructionist view of, 26–27, 29; and social change, 31–32, 117–118, 119–122, 125–126; and specialization, 6–8, 55; as stranger, 105–107, 113; technically conceived, 85–87, 92–94; training in liberal arts colleges, 86, 134–135; as transformative intellectual, 120–121, 135. *See also* name of specific person or subject, e.g., Tom; Specialization

Technical rationality: Schon's critique of, 84–85

Technocracy, 5, 17–18, 23–24

Technological growth, 3, 15, 17

Ten Years of Educational Research (Monroe), 46

Terman, Lewis, 17, 22, 43

Testing movement, 43

Thoreau, Henry David, 66

Thorndike, Edward, 17, 20, 25, 28, 87, 92

Tom, Alan, 12, 92–96, 133; compared to Counts/Cubberley, 96–97; criticism of, 98; critique of Holmes/Carnegie Reports, 99, critique of technicism in teaching, 92–94; on moral nature of teaching, 94–95; on nature of craft, 95; on NCATE standards, 95–96

Tomorrow's Teachers: A Report of the Holmes Group. See Holmes Report

Transformative intellectual, 120–121, 125, 135

Tyack, David, 11, 12, 22, 63

Tyler, Ralph, 130

The Vanishing Adolescent (Friedenberg), 70

Veblen, Thorstein, 23, 52

Voice, 118–119, 123

Vonnegut, Kurt, 65

Waller, Willard, 12, 48–55, 67, 74, 78, 88, 136; compared with Lortie, 55–58, 60, 62–63; on constraints of school culture, 50, 51, 53; and dangers of expertise, 53–54; on dangers of teacher's role, 53–54; and educational reform, 51–52, 54–55; intellectual background of, 48–50; ironies and miseries of teaching, 50–51; as a romantic, 52–53, 67

Watkins, Bruce, 85

Watson, Goodwin, 26

Weber, Max, 84

Wells, H. G., 28, 129

Wilensky, Harold L., 56

Williams, Jack, 66, 76

Winner, Langdon, 5